Paying for
COLLEGE
in the 21st Century

THE SMART AND EFFICIENT WAY
TO MAXIMIZE FINANCIAL AID

HAROLD A. GREEN, CLU® CAP®

Paying for College in the 21st Century: The Smart and Efficient Way to
Maximize Financial Aid
By Harold A. Green
HG Capital Advisors

Published in the United States by HG Capital Advisors

Library of Congress Control Number: 2014918793
HG Capital Advisors: Honolulu, HI
ISBN: 0990875806
ISBN 13: 978-0-9908758-0-2
LCCN Imprint Name: HG Capital Advisors: Honolulu, HI

Cover design, layout, and typesetting: April Carter Grant
Publisher: HG Capital Advisors

www.hgcapitaladvisors.com

This book is dedicated to the clients of HG Capital Advisors. Although there are too many to be named, I'd like to thank each one of you personally for trusting me over the years as your advisor and financial planner. Along with allowing me to help you accomplish your goals, you've allowed me to become part of your family, and for that I'm forever grateful.

Table of Contents

Foreword vii

Acknowledgments..ix

Introduction xi

Chapter 1: The High Cost of College 1

Chapter 2: The Financial-Aid Process 23

Chapter 3: Where Does the Money Come From?
Sources of Financial Aid 41

Chapter 4: How to Apply for Aid...55

Chapter 5: The Award Letter and
Leveraging for Aid..75

Chapter 6: What Can Reduce Your
Financial Aid Award? 93

Chapter 7: When to Get Started 119

What's Next? 127

About the Author 131

Foreword

Terry Shintani, MD, JD, MPH, KSJ

I remember the day, August 4, 2009, quite clearly. I arrived home from work, and as I entered the front door, my wife greeted me with extreme enthusiasm. "Terry! Guess what I got in the mail today?! A flyer to hear this guy speak on getting kids through college! We have to go!" At that time, our daughter was a sophomore in high school.

For a brief moment, I began to reflect on my own college experiences and recalled a lot of memories. I began to think of the challenges I faced. I didn't want the same for my daughter. I have a business degree from the University of Illinois, a master's degree in nutrition from Harvard University, and medical and law degrees from the University of Hawaii. Many of our friends said not to worry, that we had time because our daughter was only in the tenth grade. But my wife and I did the exact opposite. We did worry. We worried about the forms, the money, and all of the other issues that come along with sending a child off to college. When I say we worried about the money, it wasn't that we didn't have it. We simply felt there had to be a better way than just forking it over to the colleges like we've seen many other parents do. We knew there had to be some kind of expert out there who could help us. We just didn't know where to find him.

So for us, meeting Harold and his team was a godsend. As

we spent time getting to know him, one thing was for sure: he knew exactly what it was going to take to help get our daughter through college. For us it was not about the money. As a successful entrepreneur who has created the Hawaii Diet and several other health programs, set up two integrative medicine clinics and several nonprofit organizations, and published twelve books, I can confidently say I know my way around financial issues. But we lacked time and experience with the college process. Although I had attended several universities, I realized that times had changed, and so had the process. What I used to know just wasn't so. It was obsolete.

Harold was able to help us navigate the waters of higher education. As a matter of fact, he took the entire process off our hands, which freed me up to continue my work serving the community. I'm extremely grateful for having met him, and I do my best letting others know how valuable an asset he's been to us.

As you read this book, I encourage you to keep an open mind. In working with Harold, we found that much of the information we received about the college process wasn't as accurate as we thought. We learned that getting ahead of the cost of college and the college admissions process requires a head start and the right guidance. This book will definitely assist you in getting prepared to pay for college in the twenty-first century.

"E kulia i ka nu'u"—Strive for the Highest

Acknowledgments

I want to thank my wife and family for their support over the years. Making a difference in the lives of others has been no easy task. Without you, I wouldn't have been able to do it.

I'd like to thank my friend Dr. Efland Amerson for his support and words of encouragement.

And finally, I'd like to thank the team who makes HG Capital possible!

Introduction

When I began my business, HG Capital Advisors, I designed it to be a financial planning firm that assisted people in preparing and planning for successfully obtaining their big-picture dreams: home ownership, college education for their children, and retirement. But the more I worked with families, the more I saw that one of these dreams tended to disrupt the others in a major way. Paying for a child's college education was not only one of the biggest issues my clients faced in life, it was quickly becoming one of the major reasons for considering a delayed retirement. That delay, on average, was seven years!

I realized the depth of the problem when I inherited a family whose former advisor had retired. This is a very common issue today because more advisors are retiring than entering the profession. Among the three hundred thousand or so full-time financial advisors, the average age is about fifty, and 21 percent are older than sixty, according to a report from consulting firm Accenture. It's uncommon for the planner who created your plan to be around when it is time to execute it.

As I got to know this family and the details of their financial picture, what I learned dismayed and amazed me. In a meeting, I had to give them the truth as I saw the facts. I said to them, "It appears to me that your incomes are quite high, and it bothers me that you don't have as much as families with your incomes normally have."

At first I thought their previous advisor hadn't done his job, but I inquired further. "Do you mind sharing with me what happened to you over the past thirty years?"

The husband and wife looked at each other. Their response, given in unison, was sullen and quick: "It all started with paying for private school tuition," they said as if they had regretted it, which they did not.

They went on to tell me how they put their children through private school from young ages, which amounted to a hefty price tag. Now they had to pay for college as well. They looked at each other, shook their heads sadly, and said, "We wish somebody like you was around back then to help make sense of it all."

I gave them the best response I could: "I wasn't there then, but I am now, and I'm going to do everything I can from this point on to get you on track." I kept my word, but it took some time getting adjustments to work. The good news is that within the next year, both husband and wife will be retired with all of the money they're ever going to need.

The reasons this family struggled are not different from what most US families face. When you look at the financial picture of the average family, it's easy to see why paying for college is such a big problem. According to Helaine Olen in her book *Pound Foolish: Exposing the Dark Side of the Personal Finance Industry*, Americans have less than $100,000 saved in dedicated retirement accounts. She also notes that 43 percent of Americans are living paycheck to paycheck, which means they have few extra funds to devote to any kind of savings. On top of all this, salaries have stagnated, and Americans' net worth fell nearly 40 percent between 2007 and 2010. As I did more research, I found something even more astonishing: According to an analysis of a 2010 survey on consumer finances, the Employee Benefit Research Institute reported that for families with a retirement savings account, roughly two-thirds of their household net worth is locked away in those accounts!

All of this simply means that by the time a family walks through our doors, they have many questions and few answers. That leads me to the following question: If people are receiving financial advice that's in their best interest, why is it that a majority of this advice excludes preparing for the rising cost of college and focuses entirely on retirement? I'll provide an answer to that question later.

When I originally started offering college funding services, it was mainly to families of high school sophomores, juniors, and seniors. I thought these would be the families who needed my help the most. But the sad truth is, for many of those families, I found that wasn't enough time to construct a well-advised action plan and implement it before the college expenses started arriving. At this point, it's almost too late, and each year is getting worse and worse.

A lot of families may have one to two years of college tuition saved. Many of them have vague plans to take on some form of debt, but they're also hoping to curtail that with scholarships their child might earn. Sometimes they're already in a situation in which the student has been accepted to a good school but can't matriculate because of the parents' finances. Often, and this is kind of ironic, the parents make financial moves to help the family qualify for financial aid, but they end up making poor choices that actually prevent the student from getting the most free money. Simply put, they follow the wrong advice!

After countless meetings with families over the years, I finally came to the conclusion that the answer to their problem is simple: just start earlier. That, in turn, identified the problem I had: getting them to realize that starting earlier was and still is the answer! I don't just mean to start saving earlier. I mean getting informed earlier and making important decisions earlier. So I began reaching out to and working with families with younger children. There's a lot that families ought to understand, and I hope this book will help. Observing the consequences of poor decision making is what made me realize there is an enormous need for legitimate information on how to pay for or finance a college education. What many people don't realize is that there is a lot of money out there. You just have to know how to get your fair share of it.

What You'll Learn in This Book

Over the years, I designed a program that teaches what it takes for a family to get maximum funding from a college. I decided to write this book to share this important information with you and to help you prepare to work with a consultant as you navigate the financial-aid waters. It is written specifically to help middle- and upper-middle-class families get in a better position to qualify for need-based financial aid through long-term financial planning and proper decision making. This is extremely important when it comes to applying for and choosing the right college or university. Even if your family doesn't fall within the middle and upper middle class, you will still receive valuable information from this book.

However, it's the middle- and upper-middle-class families who usually get crunched out of the process and therefore have the biggest problem funding their children's educations. Why? They are in the middle, which is not necessarily a bad thing. On the extreme ends of the spectrum, families with very low or very high incomes don't have the same issues. Families with very low incomes generally are going to get aid without even trying for it, and the really wealthy don't have a funding problem because they can afford to pay for college expenses out of pocket.

I'll point out some unique challenges in this book as well. The problem for the middle- and upper-middle-class families is that they are left to contend for a dwindling pool of funds. You'll be surprised to see how, with some careful thought and planning, you can significantly increase your financial-aid award if this is your situation.

I will also educate you on the financial-aid process, and I mean the real scoop about how it all works. I'll include a brief overview of the obstacles you're going to face throughout this process. Most people labor under tremendous myths, misconceptions, and flat-out bad advice. I'll be sharing what's fake, what's real, and what you can do to prepare yourself. The truth is, there's no reason anyone needs to spend their entire life savings, or put their family into enormous debt, to pay for a college education for their child. To be honest, people share with me that they have friends who seem to be handling the situation with no problem. They ask questions and make comments like these:

- "How can they afford to pay for private school and college?"
- "They seem to be enjoying life."
- "They take vacations every year."
- "What are we doing wrong?"

- "Just how are they doing it?"

Well, they are probably incurring a lot of debt and having a lot of fights and a lot of sleepless nights. Who wants that? I wrote this book to help you avoid those. So be encouraged and continue reading! By the time you're done, you'll have a head start in bringing down the rising cost of educating your children in the twenty-first century!

—Harold A. Green

CHAPTER 1

The High Cost of College

Why is paying for college such a problem? When you consider most Americans have less than $100,000 saved in dedicated retirement accounts, and 43 percent are living paycheck to paycheck, the picture is clear: parents are too busy providing for today to plan for tomorrow. They are putting food on the table, paying for private school and/or extracurricular activities, making car payments, and caring for elderly relatives. It's hard to devote brain space to something that seems so far off in the future. Some parents leave a lot on the student's plate, thinking they will figure it out when they apply to school. But the students are scared of making wrong decisions, so they make no decision at all.

When I talk to students about their hesitation, here are the three biggest fears they share:

1. Can Mom and Dad afford it?
2. Where should I go to school? (There are 6,700 colleges to choose from—a daunting number!)
3. Can I get in? (At the really good schools competition is at an all-time high. Students are feeling a great deal of pressure to compete.)

But when students focus on that, they lose sight of the big picture, which is what? We want them to go away to college, get a four or six-year degree, get a great job, and be able to provide for themselves.

For us as parents, we want to be able to provide the best education at the lowest possible price, thereby saving thousands of dollars, and that equals success. But to be successful, we have to jump through a lot of hoops. The first hurdle we have to overcome is today's high cost of college. Why is it so expensive to send our students off to school today? Actually, it's not just expensive—it's hugely expensive, even ridiculously expensive. And if you think it seems like the issue is quickly getting worse, you're right. College costs are increasing faster than inflation rates every year. According to the College Board, tuition and fees at public four-year institutions increased 14.1 percent and rose 6 percent at private schools. Many colleges are increasing their fees by as much as 20 percent. That's staggering! But why is this happening? Why is the cost of college so steep?

Shrinking Resources

Many schools are struggling with the same market forces we deal with in our everyday lives. Changes in the stock market can and have negatively affected college endowments, an important source of funds for private schools. The same changes shrink state budgets, and that affects how much the government can help fund public schools. A 2013 *Wall Street Journal* article noted that between 1987 and 2012, in real dollars, government support for colleges declined from $8,497 to $5,906 per student.

This decline in government support should be a serious wake-up call to parents who assume a public school will automatically be less expensive. A lot of parents tell me, "We're not going to send our children to a private school. We're going to send them to a state school because a state school or public university is actually cheaper." But is it really? Let's look at some actual numbers.

If we look at the basic price tag, we see that the private school costs $52,000 a year, and the state school costs $18,000 a year. So it would appear that the parents' initial inclination is correct: the state school is cheaper. When I present this information in a live workshop I'll often ask, "How many of you would automatically enroll your student at the eighteen-thousand-dollar-a-year public school?" Half of the people in the room will raise their hands.

When I ask about it, they say the $52,000 figure is too expensive. But is it really? I will show them an example of an award letter, the document in which a school lays out how the family might expect to cover the costs of their child's attendance. One of the figures on this document will be the **expected family contribution** (EFC). This is the number that the federal government says each family can afford to pay at each school or for all of the schools they apply to. In my example, the family's EFC came in at $7,878. A family's financial-aid award is based on this simple formula:

Cost of Attendance − EFC = Need

The school will then assess how the family's need should be met. For the private school, this particular family's need is $44,889—a large sum indeed. At the public school, they would need only $10,928. That seems great, right? It's only $11,000. It certainly is a lot different than $45,000. But here's what actually happens in the financial-aid process.

School A, because it is a private university, is going to meet

100 percent of your need. School B, because it is a public school and has less means, can meet only 55 percent of your need. It leaves you short $4,917. State schools are funded by the federal government and the states themselves. Remember, we're talking about shrinking resources. This is where it's going to hit you. Here's what you're going to actually pay at each school: Your total EFC at that public university or that state school is $12,795 (The $7,878 EFC plus the unmet need of $4,917). And if your child is an out-of-state student, you're not going to pay in-state tuition. You're going to pay out-of-state tuition, and that will be higher. At the private school, your out-of-pocket contribution will remain the same as your EFC: $7,878. So which looks like the cheaper school now?

The Rising Cost of Staffing

Although schools do use graduate students and cheaper adjunct faculty, the fact remains that the salaries of professors and associate professors /teachers consistently rise and continue to be a tremendous expense. Almost two-thirds of a school's budget is allotted for salaries! Add to that the cost of benefits for those teachers and you have another nice chunk coming out of a school's coffers. The number of administrators, especially those with large salaries, has also increased. *Forbes* magazine noted that, "Between 1993 and 2007, total university expenses rose 35 percent. But administration *expenses* rose a whopping 61 percent, and instruction expenses rose 39 percent." The article also quoted a 2010 Goldwater Institute study. It found that "universities have in recent years vastly expanded their administrative bureaucracies, while in some cases actually shrinking the numbers of professors." Although enrollment rose between 1993 and 2007 by 14.5 percent, administrators employed per 100 students rose nearly 40 percent, and spending on administration per student rose by 66 percent.

Infrastructure and Maintenance

Simply put, a campus costs money—a lot. Buildings must be renovated, especially if they are old. One college in the Boston area has dedicated more than $550 million to renovate its campus buildings by 2025. Property has to be landscaped and maintained, and halls and floors have to be cleaned regularly. In recent years, some schools have increased spending on entertainment and amenities to compete for students. They have spent and sometimes borrowed millions of dollars to build luxury dorms and new dining halls. This cost has to be met somehow and it's often done through the increase of tuition.

Changes in Technology

The rise of technology in recent decades means schools have had to fund computers, wireless access systems, and IT staff members to service all of it. These upgrades, whether we realize it or not, are funded by the parents—another uptick in tuition cost. You'll notice how a company like Apple will introduce a new product every five to six months. Part of that introduction process is making everyone feel like they have to have this new hot product. Schools are no different. They want to have the latest and greatest technology to attract students to their schools. If you look at MIT's technology and then compare it to that of the University of Texas, the University of Kansas, or the University of Florida, you'll see differences. They all have various ranges of technology at their schools. Of course you expect schools such as Cal Tech, MIT, RIT, and other high-tech colleges to be ahead of the game, and there are things they do that cost money. Their tuition is high because tech companies aren't giving away technology. They aren't sampling technology. They aren't lending technology. Someone has to pay for it.

It's Not about Location

Unfortunately, it's expensive no matter where your children go to school. As I said earlier, some families believe sending their students to a state school or a local community college will significantly decrease their costs as opposed to sending them to a private school. Often, these same families also have the misconception that college costs comprise only tuition. Yes, tuition is high, but it is only the beginning. On top of that, a family is also responsible for student activity fees, books, room and board, living expenses, and transportation costs for students who incur significant costs by just traveling home for the holidays.

And there's more: often, a medical plan is not included in tuition, and you have to pay for it. There's a meal plan that parents don't think about all the way through. The average meal plan costs somewhere around $3,000 to $4,000. If your child is a student athlete, it takes a lot more money for him or her to eat. Athletes can't always eat at the scheduled time when students are supposed to go to the cafeteria and eat because they are in early-morning workouts or traveling for games. Some students are saying they can't use the meal plans that are offered if they're expected to perform like top-paid athletes. A football player has to eat 5,000, 6,000, or 7,000 calories a day just to maintain his fitness level. But once your child is on a meal plan, he or she has to eat on that meal plan unless your family has money to allow the student to eat outside of it.

By the way, if your child attends one of the schools such as the University of Florida or Oklahoma that has a big-time athletic program, you should realize that sometimes students spend a lot of money attending these extracurriculars. You'll need to consider that expense as well.

Here's an example of how costs outside of tuition can add up. One four-year private college, located in the Midwest, recently listed the following as the cost for one school year for incoming freshmen:

Tuition	$34,190
Room and board	9,490
Fees	395
Orientation	325
Total	$44,425

The school's information also notes, "In addition to direct costs, students should budget for books, supplies, and personal expenses of approximately $1,500 to $2,000." I'd say this amount is woefully low, especially when you consider that the cost of a plane ticket alone can be, at a minimum, $400 to $500.

When you add it all up, four years of college can cost $70,000 to $200,000...*or even more!* What if you have more than one child to put through school? And you'll have to add on to those costs if your child takes more than four years to graduate.

Does It Really Take Four Years?

Let's talk about that fact for a moment: most students take

more than four years to earn their degree. A *Time* magazine article recently noted, "While undergraduate education is typically billed as a four-year experience, many students, particularly at public universities, actually take five, six, or even more years to attain a degree. According to the Department of Education, fewer than 40 percent of students who enter college each year graduate within four years, while almost 60 percent of students graduate in six years. At public schools, less than a third of students graduate on time."

Note how, once again, this is more of a problem for state schools, which most parents think is the cheaper option. The reality is, *Time* states, "Overcrowded classes can make it impossible for students to fulfill degree requirements in a timely manner. And the common practice of changing majors midway through college can make a four-year degree impractical."

This situation, depending on the student, may be unavoidable, but it helps to have a good plan. *Time* quotes a Purdue executive saying students should take advantage of advisers and career counselors starting in their freshman year so that they can develop a coherent plan for their time in college, whether it is short or long. "Don't just go semester to semester," he says. "Really think ahead. If they do that right off the bat, they're much more likely to be successful and complete their studies in a reasonable amount of time."

Your "Paying for College" Plan

Actually, this same kind of thinking is exactly what I propose for financing your child's college education: You must plan and begin that planning as early as possible. What's your plan? Before you picked up this book, before you heard anything about this, what were you planning to do to pay for your child's college education? Let's pretend the bill is here today, and it is on your desk. All things being considered, your son got into the school you agreed on. He got some award money and some merit-based money. He got some financial need met, but you still have a family out-of-pocket cost of about $30,000. What is the first thing you would do? Would you take it from your savings? Would you use your home equity? Would you work a second job? Would you ask your parents or grandparents for help? Would you borrow money from a family member? What would you do? How would you pay for it? Think about your answers to these questions—write them down if you like. Now, I'd like to ask you the following about your answers:

1. **Will your plan cover the entire cost?** If you did what you were thinking about doing, would that be enough to cover everything?
2. **Could you still live the same lifestyle or better?** Would you be able to take annual vacations with your family? Could you live in the same house you're living in now? Could you drive the same car, or would you have to make a drastic cut to your lifestyle just to pay for college?
3. **Will your plan allow you to retire before the day you die?** In other words, if you borrow all of the equity in your house to pay for college, can you pay that house off before you retire, or would you have to continue working past the normal retirement age?

So, what are you supposed to do? What's the right thing to do? A lot of people initially think, "Well, OK, we've got to pay out of savings." The other option is, of course, borrowing. The third option is scholarships. And the fourth option is going to a cheaper school or not sending your child to college at all.

Let's take a look at each one of those options. But first, a word about how you might want to think about your choices. Many parents go into this with the mindset of "I don't want my child being burdened with student loans. I want to pay for as much as I can." You may have $50,000 to $100,000 saved to get your child through school, or you might have to borrow some money, or you might want to borrow some money, depending on your situation. If your investments are doing great, you may want to leverage them and borrow some money from those accounts, which will be cheaper than a bank loan. *Or you might want your child to borrow some money.* That's not a bad idea entirely, for financial reasons I outline below. Know this: statistics show nationwide that students who do take on part of the responsibility of paying for college actually do better financially once they graduate, meaning that they get better-paying jobs.

In my practice, I've seen some parents who are willing to pay 100 percent of the college cost because they don't want to burden their children. Here's what sometimes happens with these students. They graduate from college, return home, and find jobs that don't pay much because they don't need much. In contrast, the students who have to borrow money or take out loans end up taking on better-paying jobs so they can meet their obligations. For example, there was a student who went through our program. His parents paid some of the costs, but he ended up borrowing money to get through graduate school, and he eventually became a physical therapist. Contrast that with the student who went off to college, had everything paid for him, and then took a job teaching that didn't pay as much.

I'm not putting down teaching, but there's a big difference between the two. It's just something to think about.

Savings

We all know we're supposed to be saving, right? Saving for retirement, saving for vacations, saving for college education. Not everyone had the opportunity over the past seventeen years to set aside all the money to pay for college, but some people were able to set money aside. They have it in a Uniform Gift to Minors Act (UGMA) account. They may have it in a 529 plan. There may be even money in trust accounts from Grandma or Grandpa, but the bottom line is, you might have some money set aside to get your children through school. Saving is supposed to be a good thing. It's supposed to help. But when you're saving for college, depending on how you do it, that's not always true. If, for example, you have saved $20,000 in your child's name, you could potentially be losing about $7,000 in free money. According to the Free Application for Federal Student Aid, which everyone must complete when applying for financial aid, that kind of money will go against you and your family contribution at 35 percent. If you have saved money in your own name, that's going to count against you at 5.6 percent. This simply means that a family's resources are counted in the federal formula. Parent income counts heavily percentage-wise in the formula.

Often there is a small asset protection allowance, but it's certainly not much. The asset protection allowance is the amount of funds you are allowed to have that is not included in the financial-aid formula. Let's say you're $100,000 over the allowance, so that's another $5,600 you're potentially giving up in free money. That includes federal grants and scholarships, state grants and scholarships, and any funds from the biggest source of free money—the schools themselves. So if you've saved money, you really need to know what you should or shouldn't be doing about that money legally before you get involved in this process. Some people have approached me and said, "You know what? We've done a really good job of setting money aside, or it was gifted to us, but we just want to go after the free scholarship stuff. If we don't get that kind of money, then we'll just have to pay out of pocket." I say you're being shortsighted. There are ways to get more money, free money from the federal government, the states, and the schools. Why on earth would you not want to take a look at that based on your specific situation? A word of caution here: I'm not saying that if you have all of the money to pay for college, you should try to hide it so that you can qualify for financial aid. What I am saying is this there could be better things to do with that money that provide a greater future benefit versus wasting it unnecessarily on tuition just because you have it. The caveat here is that it depends on your situation.

Borrowing

Most families are going to have to borrow money to get their children through school. But before you consider borrowing money to pay for your child's education, you should know the answers to three questions:

1. How much are you supposed to borrow?
2. Who are you going to borrow it from?
3. How long is it going to take you to pay it back?

There are different types of loans out there. There are **fed-**

eral loans, **Stafford** loans, **unsubsidized** loans, subsidized loans. There are **Parent PLUS** loans. There are **home equity** loans. There are **cash out refinance** loans. There are even loans on your **401(k)**. As a matter of fact, the max you can borrow on a 401(k) these days is about $50,000—possibly not enough to cover all four years of your child's college education.

For the most part, though, loans fall into two groups:

- **Federal student loans:** These loans are funded by the federal government.
- **Private student loans:** These loans are nonfederal loans made by a *lender* such as a bank, credit union, state agency, or school.

The US Department of Education has two federal student loan programs. (These descriptions are posted on the department's government website):

- The William D. Ford Federal *Direct Loan* Program is the largest federal student loan program. Under this program, the US Department of Education is your *lender*. Four types of direct loans are available:
  - **Direct subsidized loans** are made to eligible undergraduate students who demonstrate financial need to help cover the costs of higher education at a college or career school.
  - **Direct unsubsidized loans** are made to eligible undergraduate, graduate, and professional students, but in this case, the student does not have to demonstrate financial need to be eligible for the loan.

- **Direct PLUS loans** are made to graduate or professional students and parents of dependent undergraduate students to help pay for education expenses not covered by other financial aid.
- **Direct consolidation loans** allow you to combine all of your eligible federal student loans into a single loan with a single *loan servicer*.

- The **Federal Perkins Loan Program** is a school-based loan program for undergraduates and graduate students with exceptional financial need. Under this program, the school is the lender.

How much money can I borrow in federal student loans?

- If you are an undergraduate student:
  - Up to $5,500 per year in Perkins Loans depending on your financial need, the amount of other aid you receive, and the availability of funds at your college or career school
  - $5,500 to $12,500 per year in Direct Subsidized Loans and Direct Unsubsidized Loans depending on certain factors, including your year in college
- If you are a graduate student:
  - Up to $8,000 each year in Perkins Loans depending on your financial need, the amount of other aid you receive, and the availability of funds at your college or career school
  - Up to $20,500 each year in direct unsubsidized loans
  - The remainder of your college costs not covered by other financial aid in Direct PLUS loans. Note: A credit check is required for a PLUS loan.

- If you are a parent of a dependent undergraduate student:
    - The remainder of your child's college costs that
      are not covered by other financial aid. Note: A
      credit check is required for a parent loan (called a
      PLUS loan).

This is a lot to take in, but the only way you're going to know
how to borrow money is by fully understanding your specific
situation. When we work with families, their situation tends to
fit one of three categories:

Category One: Your family can go to any school and
get the maximum free money hands down because of
low income.

Category Two: Your family will be able to go to some
schools and get some free money. Other schools are
going to tell you, "Get out of here. Take a hike." Well,
not quite, but you get the idea!

Category Three: These are the families who think
or tell us they are making way too much money and
they're not going to qualify for any need-based financial aid whatsoever. So they don't even apply.

Understanding your situation will help you make better decisions even if you are in a position to help your child. You'll have
a better idea of how to borrow and why to borrow a certain way.
For all of your willingness to take on the burden of paying for
the college education, sometimes it just makes more financial
sense to let your child do the borrowing. For example, let's say
your student goes off to college and becomes a nurse through

a nursing program. You, as the parents, borrow all of the money from a Parent PLUS Loan, $80,000, for your child to finish nursing school because you want to pay for the education.

Your child graduates at last, and she goes to work for an employer that offers loan forgiveness. You're all excited about that loan forgiveness—until you learn that the loan had to be in your child's name, not yours, for it to be forgiven. You're frustrated because back when you started the financial-aid process, you were told not to borrow in your child's name because it was a bad thing to do. Now you are stuck having to pay back the loan. An aside: I don't mean to be morbid here, but you should know that if your child should pass away prematurely, the loan will not be forgiven. For this reason, I encourage my clients to have life insurance on themselves if they borrow money and on the students who borrow money so the debt is paid in the event of a tragedy.

Scholarships

Last year, families received more than $160 billion in the form of financial aid. Can you guess how much of that money came from scholarships? And we're talking about private scholarships. Would you say 5 percent, 10 percent, 30 percent, maybe even 90 percent? The fact is that about 6.7 to 7 percent of all the free money given out came from private scholarships. That's it. If you want to know more about scholarships, visit www.fastweb.com. Have your children do all of the research on scholarships because honestly, it's their responsibility to try to find as much money as they can get on their own before parents step in and pay whatever is not covered.

A note of warning: companies that bill themselves as "scholarship search services" are not worth the money. Don't pay for them. Sometimes they can be a complete rip-off. But there are legitimate scholarship services out there. You just have to find out which ones are. We always tell the parents to talk to their local high school guidance counselors about them, just to be on the safe side.

Before we go any further, let's talk about what the word "scholarship" means. The definition has changed a lot in recent years. There are private scholarships. Coca-Cola has a scholarship. Burger King has a scholarship. Colleges also have scholarships. We once thought of a scholarship as money awarded to recognize excellence in academics or sports. Nowadays, though, a scholarship can be based on need. Schools such as MIT, Columbia, Harvard, or Yale might provide some free, need-based aid and call it a scholarship, but this is a misnomer. It's not really a scholarship. When you hear the word "scholar," you're thinking "smart student" or "merit," whereas these schools are actually giving out need-based grants. It's *need-based* financial aid versus *merit-based* financial aid.

In fact, a lot of the top schools aren't giving out merit-based financial aid anymore because of a leveling of the playing field: all of the students are smart. On those grounds alone, all would qualify for merit-based financial aid. So if they gave your student a merit scholarship over mine and they both happen to have the same, perhaps even perfect, SAT and ACT scores, what would you call that? Discrimination. The only way schools can avoid discrimination is to give out money on a need basis. You can't argue with need because the federal government determines need. If you argue with that, you're going to argue with the government.

So in this section, I'm actually talking about private scholarships. This 6.7 percent of funding comes from places like

Coca-Cola, the Shriners, Starbucks, and the like. Later in this book, we will look at how these scholarships will affect your financial-aid letter and how they can make your situation worse than if you had never gotten the scholarship. For now, just know it will be a small figure in your calculations of how you'll pay for college.

Not Going to College

Once upon a time, not going to college was a valid option. There was a time in the United States when there were many job opportunities in factories and high-level service industries that allowed workers without college degrees to provide their families with middle-class and even upper-middle-class lifestyles. Such jobs have all but disappeared. Today the fact of the matter is, in many cases, that when a person applies for a job, the first thing employers look for is whether or not he or she has a college diploma. So not going to college at all is no longer a viable option.

I have to admit that some people do luck out. "How?" you may be wondering. Let's take a look at some of the careers out there. The Armed Forces have been a great avenue for some individuals. However, please keep in mind that it is the exception, not the rule. There are other honorable careers as well: firefighter, police officer, flight attendant, and plumber are a few examples. However, to climb the ranks in these fields today, a degree is essential because upper-level management will require a certain knowledge level. The higher you climb, the greater the amount of education you need. Schools such as the University of Phoenix and Kaplan University, which offer online courses, are becoming extremely popular because many people are going back to college after realizing they need more education. With all things being considered, I'm going to assume that if you're reading this book, you and your son or daughter are probably not looking at any of the careers I just mentioned.

Also, personally, I think there are a lot of things you can't put a price tag on that students learns while in college. They gain self-confidence and enhanced employment opportunities, which will allow them to make more money. For many students, college is their first taste of independence, of living away from home. They can also increase their network for both career and social benefits.

But before parents reap these benefits, I want them to really understand the "why." Why are they sending their children to college? We discuss this constantly, often via newsletters and other media pieces we send to parents to keep them informed and focused on why they are making the effort to work on their finances.

The primary reason most parents send their kids off to college is to do what? Prepare them to get jobs. For a lot of students, it's not really about, "Should I go to college or not?" It's more about, "What should I do? What should I study? What major should I take on?" I believe this is not forward-thinking enough. We have to look at the end goal from the very beginning. We have to look at this with the student and have the student ask, "First of all, how much money do I want to make? Better yet, how much money do I think I'm going to need to live on every single month?" We can proceed from there and keep asking questions such as, "What kind of lifestyle do I want to have? Do I want a nice home? Do I want a nice car? What are my values?" That's how you choose a career. You choose a field perhaps by asking, "What am I passionate about?" and then you try to find that career that's going to fulfill that passion, but at the same time, meet your lifestyle.

The student might also take these factors into consideration: "Do I want to live close to Mom and Dad? Do I want to stay in the same city I'm in now and raise my family here? What are the job opportunities like here? What are they going to be like in five years, ten years, fifteen years?" These are all questions a student will have to answer before he or she can even start looking at a major or even a college. Once they figure out those values, then they can begin to look at questions such as, "OK, I love the arts. That's my passion. I'm a great performer, so where should I go to college? What college has the best program for that? Which college is going to give me the best internship program to help me land that great job because it's so competitive out there?"

Once the student narrows down the choices, then he or she can choose the major. A lot of people make the mistake of first thinking, "What should I major in?" when they have no idea what their lifestyle is going to be like. More than 50 percent of Americans surveyed say they hate their jobs. It's actually 80 percent according to Deloitte's Shift Index survey. Those surveyed said that if they could choose to do anything else, if it would make them the same amount of money to cover their lifestyle, they said they would make a change. I believe failing to think of lifestyle first when choosing a profession led them to this dissatisfaction.

By the way, I don't mean that if your child decides to become an artist that you should support her for the rest of her life. But that's what can happen if you say to your child, "OK, great! Follow your passion!" You'll be writing blank checks for a long time. Can you afford that?

Instead, here's another way. I did this with my own children. I advised them to get a job in an area where they have the greatest amount of skill. I suggested that they find something they're really good at and can pretty much do with their eyes closed. However, it must, in some way or fashion, benefit society or our planet. They can build a financial foundation with that career and if they have passions elsewhere, they can fulfill them in an extracurricular role. My daughter loves to paint and illustrate. I said, "Well, if you want to be an artist, guess what? Either you become a highly skilled and highly paid professional who can afford all the utensils and all the canvases you'll need for your art and then practice it in your spare time, or find something easier to do and then paint." If she does the latter, that's fine, but she has to realize that her way of life, as she currently knows it, will forever be changed. Until she becomes a star with her art, she will have an altered lifestyle. If that's what she wants, then that's what she wants.

We have to approach it using a common-sense method and from a responsible point of view. I'm telling my children that they're making an adult choice, and it's a choice they are paying for. I've observed too many parents funding that choice, and they think they have to. But in reality, they don't. I know a man who can't retire until after the age of seventy because that's what he did: he let the student decide. He wanted what made his child happy. Well, his child is happy. Happy doing not much with her life, and he's paying for it. You see, he never explained to his daughter the ground rules under which she was to achieve that happiness. Nor did he place any expectations on her.

Moving On

So we've established that the cost of college is high. Some of the cost has to do with the way schools are run and financed. Some of the cost has to do with poor decision making on the part of the families sending their students to college. However, the structure of our society has made college, for the most part, a necessary expense if we aspire to a certain future for our children.

Now let's look at the process that these institutions and the government designed to help families handle this financial burden.

CHAPTER 2

The Financial-Aid Process

For most families, the financial-aid process is shrouded in mystery. They enter it like a patch of dense fog on the road and come out on the other side with an award letter in hand featuring a bunch of numbers and a decision made about their future without a clear understanding of how they got there. Who made the decision? How did they come up with these numbers? For being such an important part of sending a child to college, parents simply know too little about the financial-aid process. What they do know is often, at best, partially inaccurate or at worst, completely wrong.

Because of such rampant confusion, I believe a good place to begin is to dispel a few myths. As you read through the following information, I encourage you to think about whether any of these myths is one you believe. If it is, think about how you would have been thrown off track by this misinformation. Would you have not applied for financial aid? Would you have made a wrong financial move? It's good to think this way because it will help you see how big a difference having the right support and the right information can make.

Myth #1: Our Income Is Too High

Before they look at a financial-aid form (or even before they know what one looks like!), a lot of people automatically think they are disqualified from the process because they believe their income is too high. I always ask the question,

"What is too high?" Is $50,000 too much? Is $100,000 too much? What about $150,000, $200,000, or $300,000? I find it interesting how none of my clients, when I begin working with them, can answer this question, yet many of them have already made this assumption for their family. What is the answer? The real answer is that we don't know—at least not at first. It all depends on the schools the families apply to. Every school has different requirements and different ways of dividing up its financial-aid budget. So the point here is this: don't count yourself out.

Myth #2: My Child's Grades Are Too Low

When I teach this material in my live workshops, I always ask the students in attendance, "What grades are too low to get you into college? Is a D too low? Is a C too low? What is too low?" A lot of times, I'll get the answer in the form of a grade point average: 3.0. The thinking is that if your grade point average is lower than a 3.0, you can't go to college. But that's not true. Actually, there are a lot of colleges that will accept a C student and sometimes even a D student because they know everybody needs an opportunity to go to college. That's the truth. Now here's an ugly truth: if a child is a C or a D student, Mom and Dad are going to pay for it. There are no scholarships. There is no financial aid for the types of schools willing to take on such students. The parents are just going to have to pay for it because they know their child needs an education.

Myth #3: I Can't Get Aid because I Own a Home

This is a big one. Many people think that because they have too much equity in their home, they're not going to qualify for any type of need-based financial aid. But the Free Application for Federal Student Aid (FAFSA) form doesn't ask about your home equity. The only time you have to provide home equity information is when you're filling out the CSS PROFILE form, which I'll get into a little bit later. The point, once again, is that this kind of detail varies according to the school. Many of them do take into account the fact that your home is an asset and that it can be used for college. Why? Because for many, many years, that's what your predecessors have done: they have taken equity from their homes to pay for a child's education. I've heard stories of people remortgaging their house one, two, three, and even four times to get their children through college. This trend has created an expectation among colleges that the home is fair game. People use home equity for other types of purchases: renovations, stock purchases, cars. Why not use it for education? It is an investment, right? That's how the thinking goes.

Myth #4: Aid Is Only for Special Groups

I did not post a photo of myself anywhere in this book, but just in case you're wondering, I'm black. And because of that, when I was growing up, I was told, "Hey, you don't need to worry about paying for college because you're in a special group. You're black. Blacks tend to get all kinds of financial aid. You can qualify for the max free money." So I thought I would get to go to college inexpensively just because I'm black.

Of course there were grades I had to earn and forms I had to fill out to get this free money. In my senior year in high school, I went to my college counselor and said, "I'm a minority student. What can I get in the form of scholarship?"

She said, "Well, let's apply for several scholarships for you."

I filled out the scholarship paperwork. My grades were pretty good, so I thought I had a great chance of getting into college and having it paid for. But that's not exactly what happened. At the end of my senior year, I got the results back from the scholarship applications, and the news wasn't great. I got beat out for one scholarship by another student who was a female and a different nationality from a different country. At that time, she was considered more of a minority than I was, so I was passed over for that scholarship. The same thing happened to a lot of other students. As a matter of fact, most of the girls in our class who applied for scholarships got more money than the guys who applied for them. They say scholarships are only for special groups, but you can never be certain how you'll be viewed when you apply, so that's not necessarily true. It depends on your situation. Again, don't count yourself in or out before you look further into the process.

Myth #5: It's an Easy Process

For some reason, it seems that schools would like you to believe the financial-aid process is easy: You just fill out some forms and send them in, and then boom, bam, you're done. When I discuss this myth in my workshop, I'll ask my audience how many of them have gone through the process before. A few people will raise their hands. Sometimes they've already gone through it with two or even three children. I'll ask, "Well, what do you think about the process? Was it easy?"

Their answer? "Heck, no! It's not easy. It's not easy at all."

I'll ask, "So it's pretty time-consuming, right?"

They say, "Yeah." They go on to point out that you almost need a CPA or a tax professional to fill out forms for you. The forms require data from your taxes as well as some pretty complicated financial information. Most people have no clue how to organize any of this, let alone put the information down on paper in the most accurate, beneficial way. It can be a daunting process. Filling out the form isn't all that matters; what's really important is what you put on the form. There are tax breaks such as solar credits, energy credits, and education credits. If you don't know how to take advantage of those, you're going to lose out on thousands and thousands of dollars. Your financial-aid form is the same way.

Do you know what assets actually count against you on the financial-aid form? Do you know the gray areas? Do you know the housing allowances? Do you know how to negotiate the gray areas like you do with your taxes? You have to know how to take advantage of the loopholes. Anyone can sit down and punch in their numbers based on what they see on forms, but there's a lot more to it. Planning is required, and once you get the planning done, you'll have a different outcome.

I'll give an example. Let's say two families have identical assets and incomes of $100,000 a year. If we did college financial planning for Family A, but we didn't work with Family B, guess what? Family A's expected contribution to college costs may come out to be, say, $10,000, whereas Family B's comes out to $25,000. That's a $15,000 disparity. Yet they both have the same income and the same assets. What's the difference? One family took advantage of the gray areas. The other family just left the important decisions and planning up to school representatives or other misinformed advice, and that's what they got as a result.

Myth #6: School Representatives Can Help with the Process

So that we can better examine this myth, we have to understand how school representatives fit in the financial-aid process. First, let's think about our goal. What are we attempting to do here? We want to figure out how to apply for financial aid, get our children through four years of college, and pay the least amount of money for it, right?

Now, consider this: Is a school representative actually qualified to help you make this financial decision? You're going to receive your financial award letter from the school, and it will say, for example, "We're going to give you only $10,000 for school. You have to come up with $30,000." Would you then take that letter to a school counselor and ask, "Mr. or Mrs. Jones, do you think I should accept this award letter?" Is he or she truly the right person to help you make this decision? If that person says, "Yes," guess what? You're on the hook for coming up with $30,000.

Then you might say, "Well, Mr. or Mrs. Jones, how do you think we can come up with this money?"

The person would respond with, "Well, we don't do that. You need to sit down and talk to your financial planner and figure out how to come up with that thirty thousand dollars."

But here's the thing: What if there was something you could've done to avoid having to pay $30,000 in the first place and the school representative has no idea about it? This is precisely my point. The counselor is not someone who is qualified to help you make a financial decision, and paying for college is a financial decision. I know some colleges may argue with this, but the fact is, school representatives are in the business of getting money from you; they're not in the business of giving money to you. Their job is admissions, admissions, admissions. As far as how to pay for it, that's a whole different ball of wax.

Families try to have financial discussions with high school counselors, too, but their job is also admissions. Their job is to help your child get in to college. Yet families rely on them as their sole source of information about the whole financial-aid process. Why? Because most people procrastinate, pro-crastinate, procrastinate, and finally they say, "OK, now we've got a senior in high school. Let's go talk to the school and see what they can do." But you had seventeen years to figure this out, and now you're at that crucial point. At your school there may be as many as four hundred students to one counselor. There are only 365 days in a year (and only about 180 days in a school year), and this counselor may see only one or two students a day because the students are so busy with their schedules they can't make time to come in. Are you sure you want to talk only to this one person (if you can get an ap-pointment) for three months to figure out what to do for the rest of your child's life? That's not going to cut the mustard. Unfortunately, that's where a lot of people are.

The Upshot?

I hope you'll consider all of this information and not rely on what you think you know. You may be unnecessar-ily counting yourself out of financial aid or simply making the wrong assumptions. Take the time to get the right help and learn the facts as they pertain to your unique situation. Reading this book is a great start. It will also help to know where you stand in terms of the types of families who seek college financial planning assistance. Basically, there are only three categories of families:

1. Families with total financial need
2. Families with partial financial need
3. Families who may not get any financial aid.

As you can imagine, the situation of each type of family can be quite different. I'll go into some detail here and explain.

1. Families with total financial need

These are the families who are going to get financial aid wherever their child goes to school. Everything must be done 100 percent accurately and *on time* for these people to get the maximum free money and fewer loans. But here are the difficulties I've seen with such families. They'll come in and say, "You know what? We can't afford college. One year of college costs more than what we actually make. We've been telling our children, 'If you're going to go to college, you've got to join the military or work for a year and save some money.' We just can't pay for it."

These families usually don't have any experience with higher education. They typically don't have a professional certificate, a bachelor's degree, or a master's degree. They have the basic high school education, but sometimes they don't even have that. They may have dropped out of school and gotten decent jobs working at factories and so on. They don't think they can send a kid to college, but these families are the ones who qualify for the most free money. The biggest challenge I've seen is this: students from these families tend to have low grades, but you may find one or two families whose children have excellent grades. But the families are still under the assumption that they can't afford school. Well, based on good grades and on the family's financial situation, they can get money pretty much anywhere.

Another problem is that they don't submit their forms in a timely manner. They may have a fear of filling out forms or a fear of processes. They don't want to get involved in it and may even be suspicious of an institution asking so many personal questions. Sometimes they leave it up to the students to fill out the forms, but a young person isn't necessarily the best person to count on for getting financial-aid forms completed.

Here is an example. We had one student come in who was part of a single-parent family. The mother was receiving a little child support, but not a whole lot. Her child is a very bright kid, definitely college material. But the mother never filed her FAFSA form. She just assumed a school would give them free money because they're poor, and she wouldn't have to do a thing. She was only half right. The school that her child applied to was indeed one of these schools that would've given her 100 percent of her need in free money and grants—*if her family had sent the forms in on time.* They didn't. They just blew the process, and her child ended up staying at home and attending a local community college when that child could've gone to one of the best schools in the country and received a lot of free money. That's a sad story but, unfortunately, it's a common one in this category of families.

2. Families with partial financial need

These are the families who will get some money from some schools. Other schools may turn them down, but it depends on how the family's income and assets are positioned. And often a family's place of residence is taken into consideration. In certain parts of the country, you have to make more than $100,000 just to be able to put food on the table. If you live in New York, certain parts of California, or even in Hawaii, and one parent is your average nurse and the other parent is a teacher, they could have a household income of almost $200,000 between the two of them because that's what salaries are like in those parts of the country. So they'll fall into this category in which, depending on their income and assets, they'll get some money. In other schools, like I said earlier, they're not going to get anything.

The majority of the families who come in to see us are in this category, and they usually have one or two children for whom they're paying private school tuition. They have a house. They have some money in individual retirement accounts (IRAs) and 401(k)s, but they don't have all of the money it's going to take to get their children through college. We sit down with them and figure out how to position them properly to get more money at certain schools. Then we help them target the schools that are the right fit for their particular situation.

3. Families who may not get any financial aid

Some families do make too much money to qualify for financial aid, but sometimes the schools will still make them go through the paperwork process to see who's more eligible for the merit-based money. I know that may seem odd, but let me explain. Let's say two students are identical on paper. They have the same GPAs, the same SAT scores, and a similarly impressive list of extracurricular activities. They are so off-the-chart as students that they just pop off the paper to college administrators.

How do you know which one of these students is more deserving of a merit-based scholarship? Do the university's financial-aid officers just put their names in a hat and draw one out? No. Normally what they will do is call the parents and say, "We need you to fill out these financial-aid forms so that your child can be considered for this scholarship." They may not say it that way, or they may just have you fill out forms and submit them. You may not even know what the forms are for, but sometimes that is what it's for.

The bigger issue, though, with these families in the third category is that in our country, we consider them rich. They're making a certain income, but most don't realize how many more issues they have to deal with. The biggest problem I see with these families is that they do have the income, but they have no money left over at the end of the day. Usually, they're trying to keep up with the lifestyle they have grown accustomed to. They have the nice cars, the nice homes, the great incomes, but the lifestyle is just killing them. As a matter of fact, I've seen them have way less money than the people who were in the previous two categories. And so, when we sit down with these families, we have to take a lot of different things into consideration because these families are going to be paying for college on an after-tax basis, not on a pretax basis. With their high incomes, they pay taxes and then they have very little left over to pay for college because their EFC is not a pretax number. The universities do take a little bit of the taxes these families pay into account, but not a ton because the family's EFC is still astronomical.

For example, let's say your income is $150,000. After you

file your tax return, it is determined that your net tax rate for federal and state is a combined 9 percent after credits and deductions. That means you'll pay $13,500 in total taxes and will be left with $136,500. However, the EFC is calculated based on a number closer to $150,000. If the university assesses your income at 25 percent of available assets used for college, your EFC would be roughly $37,500! Ouch! And you still owe taxes. So after paying $13,500 in taxes and $37,500 for the first year of college, your family will have about $109,000 left. To make matters worse, you don't catch a break for the IRA/401(k) contributions because they are thrown back in on top of your adjusted gross income. It's no wonder that families are struggling to stay ahead of the rising cost of college.

Eligibility and You

The next thing we're going to look at is your eligibility for financial aid. How do the schools determine who's eligible and who's not? Let's start with the basic formula that is at the heart of the financial-aid process:

COA – EFC = need

COA stands for **cost of attendance**. It includes the price of books, tuition, room, board, and a lot of other things you don't see. For example, I just listed tuition, books, room, and board, but what's missing from that list? A meal plan! The cost of an average meal plan can range anywhere from $3,000 to $5,000 a year, and it's not included in this cost-of-attendance number.

When you get your breakdown for the cost of college, you

have to make sure you understand what's missing. You'll have to ask yourself questions such as, "Is my child an athlete? How much is he going to eat? How much extra money do we have to allot for that?" Or if you live in California and you send your child to college at NYU, the airfare, which probably will be at a premium because he or she will most likely be flying during a holiday season, will have to be included in your budget as well. There are so many more things that are in this total cost of attendance that we're not even factoring in: a new laptop, new phones, and winter clothes. How many times are you going to go visit your child in college? Are you going to send care packages? How often? Those are things that you really need to think about and add into your budget.

The next thing we have is EFC, **expected family contribution**. As mentioned, this is the amount the federal government says you can comfortably afford to pay for your child's education. Let me ask you a few questions: These are the same people who are telling you how much income tax you have to pay, right? I'll answer that one for you: yes. Do you think the amount of tax you pay is fair? Most people say no. So my next question is this: why on earth would you think that your EFC number is going to come out to be a fair number? It probably won't be fair because here's what they base it on: your income, your assets, your child's income, your child's assets, the ages of your family members, the number of people in your family who are in school, and a host of other different factors. Every family will have different life experiences that don't get factored into the equation. Some families will have assets gifted to them over time, such as a home. Let's assume a family has a home that is mortgage-free. The value doesn't matter because the federal formula won't include it.

Let's also assume that this family's household income is a combined $65,000 and their net effective tax rate is zero. If we run that $65,000 through the 25 percent calculation, their EFC should come out to $16,250 right? Wrong! Because their income is below a certain threshold, their EFC comes out to be—get this—$7,153! Isn't there something wrong with this picture? This family appears to have a greater *need* than the family in the previous example, but do they? Let's continue the discussion of *need*.

At this point, I highly recommend that you not even proceed with trying to figure where to send your children off to school until you figure out what your situation is and exactly what all of these numbers mean for your family. Remember, COA – EFC = need. You have to ask yourself what you can really afford. A better question would be what are you really eligible for, and do you know how to go about getting it? In other words, what do you *need*, and how will you get that *need* met? I believe a family should pay only its fair share and not a penny more.

You must know what these numbers are. Without knowing, you will be absolutely lost. There will be no way to make heads or tails of the situation. So how can you plan for it? You simply can't. I'm all for planning, but I don't condone planning in the blind. Here's a good example of blind planning. Every single year, people sit down and plunk millions of dollars into IRAs and 401(k)s. Why do they do that? Because they are trying to plan for retirement.

First of all, they have no clue what they will really need, nor do they know any of the other factors that go into creating a solid plan that's guaranteed to work every single time without fail. Here's what I mean. Out of their annual salaries, anywhere from 3 to 15 percent is being contributed to some kind of "retirement vehicle," and many people have no clue of whether the money will be there when they need it. They have no real idea what the tax rate is going to be. All of these things they just don't know. But, it's done regardless, right? Why? The honest answer is because the financial industry is telling them to do it. I hear this argument quite often: there are no student loans for retirement or financial aid for retirement, so you have to take care of yourself. The students can borrow their way through school. *Really!?* I'm not saying don't plan or save for retirement, but statistics show that as many as 95 percent of people who retire will not have enough money in retirement, in spite of all their best efforts. That statement alone could be another book, but I will get back to my point of trying to figure out your eligibility for financial aid and how to go about getting all the money you qualify for. All roads point back to the FAFSA.

Now, the thing about filling out the FAFSA form is this: people who complete the form and don't get awarded financial aid from a college for the first student usually will never reenter the process for the second child. What do I mean by that? Well, according to the formula **(COA – EFC = need)**, if I have two students in school, I would be entitled to more. But if I'm turned off or feel like I got jilted, why would I want to go through the hassle of providing all of my personal information to no avail? Because the expectation is there that I'm just going to waste my time. Here's what you could be missing out on.

Let's say, for example, that your cost of attendance is $40,000 at the University of Washington. They run all the numbers, and your EFC comes out to be $10,000. How much need are you eligible for? Well, $40,000 minus $10,000 equals $30,000. So you fill out all the forms and send them in but receive no financial aid from the University of Washington whatsoever for your oldest child's freshman year.

Now, let's assume you had your children a year apart. So you have a freshman who is going to be a sophomore in college and also a senior in high school who's going to be a freshman in college. Let's also assume that you sit through a number of financial-aid seminars or workshops. Then you spend the time and effort going through this whole process and get absolutely nothing for your oldest child. Therefore, you're going to think that you won't get anything for the second child, either. Maybe your income and assets go up a little, but nothing extremely significant. Nothing else has really changed, so why in the world would you go back into this process, anyway? Chances are you won't. What if something could have been done to improve your situation and chances of getting more funding, and you didn't know about it? Here's the deal.

You have two children in college. Your EFC should drop based on the formula. But what if you didn't know that? Imagine this. Your new cost of attendance is $80,000, and because you have two children in school, your EFC should drop down to about $5,000. How much aid are you eligible for now? Your need is $70,000, but you didn't fill out the forms. You didn't go back into the process.

You don't call the school to figure out what happened, and you end up trying to figure out how to pay $70,000 out of cash flow and assets. You do that for three years. Seventy times three is $210,000. That is the amount you're going to leave on the table. I've seen that scenario time and time again. Some people skip the process automatically because somebody told them they don't qualify, or they think they make too much money to qualify for a need-based aid. Let me give you another example.

John and Jerry both work at the same company. They've both been there for about twenty years and are approaching retirement. They have identical incomes. As a matter of fact, they live in the same community a couple of houses apart from each other. Jerry's son was a couple of years older that John's daughter, so Jerry went through the process first.

Jerry says, "Look, we went through this process. We didn't get any financial aid, so I don't know what you guys are going to do." John automatically assumes that Jerry did *everything* right, no questions asked. He goes home and tells his wife, "I just talked to Jerry, and they put their daughter through school and got no financial aid. Looks like we might be in the same boat, honey. We're probably not going to get anything, so if our daughter is to attend college, we're probably going to have to borrow the money."

I heard a story about a family who didn't make a lot of money, but an advisor told them that they made too much money to qualify for financial aid. As a result, they took on $80,000 in loans.

After digging further, I found out that that should've never happened to that family. Based on the wrong advice, they will probably have to suffer through this situation unnecessarily for quite some time.

Please don't take what I'm about to say the wrong way, but when it comes to families getting hurt by bad advice or incorrect information, it bothers me. It bothers me a lot. Let me share this: if you've gone to somebody for help with your child's college funding situation and they haven't shared any of this information with you, you have to consider switching advisors. Here's why.

It's impossible to know where you stand moneywise at any particular school without knowing this information first. And without this info, you can't plan. So if you have a plan that didn't take this information into consideration, is it really any good? No. Without it, your plan will fail! Some people share with me that they don't plan because they are not sure if their child will even attend college. My response to that is, "Do you really have much of a choice in today's world?"

CHAPTER 3

Where Does the Money Come From? Sources of Financial Aid

When you apply for financial aid, you're essentially asking to dip into a pot of funds that have been made available from various sources to help families pay for college. It helps to know how much aid is available—in other words, how big is the pot? How much are you competing for when you submit your financial-aid forms? You'll also want to know where this money comes from. Why? Because the answer will help you know where to focus your efforts so that you can get the biggest amount of free money possible.

The pot is actually a pretty big one. Believe it or not, more than $200 billion dollars of aid is available. That would pay for a lot of textbooks, wouldn't it? All of these funds are available to most families. You only have to know where to get it. Just so you know where to look, this is a breakdown[1] of the sources of this money. I think you'll find it interesting:

- Federal loans: 44 percent
- Collegiate resources: 20 percent
- Federal grants: 12 percent
- State government resources: 7 percent
- Tuition tax credits: 7 percent
- Veterans Administration: 3 percent

---

1   Don't Miss Out: The Ambitious Guide To Financial Aid, by Anna & Robert Leider, 30th Edition, Octomeron Associates.

- Employer-paid tuition: 4 percent
- Private sources: 3 percent

Notice that last one, private sources, and its share of the pie, 3 percent. I'll get back to it a little later. For now, let's take a closer look, top to bottom, at the resources these institutions provide.

Federal Government

The federal government, through the US Department of Education, is very much in the business of helping students afford an education. However, a lot of people are under the mistaken impression that it does so for free. Most people, when they think of federal funds for college, think of grants. But as you can see by the percentages listed above, the biggest chunk of money the government provides is in the form of loans. The details of how these loans are disbursed and repaid vary, and it's important to know the difference before you apply. You can learn more about all federal programs online at studentaid.ed.gov. Here are the basics.

The US Department of Education has two federal **student loan** programs:

The **William D. Ford Federal Direct Loan Program** is the largest federal student loan program. Under this program, the US Department of Education will act as your lender. Four types of direct loans are available:

1. **Direct subsidized loans** are loans made to eligible undergraduate students who demonstrate financial need to help cover the costs of higher education at a college or career school. Direct subsidized loans have slightly better terms than some other loans. Your

school determines the amount you can borrow, and the amount may not exceed your financial need. The US Department of Education pays the interest on a direct subsidized loan:

— While you're in school at least half-time
— For the first six months after you leave school (referred to as a "grace period")
— During a period of deferment (a postponement of loan payments).

2. **Direct unsubsidized loans** are made to eligible undergraduate, graduate, and professional students, but in this case, the student does not have to demonstrate financial need to be eligible for the loan. Your school determines the amount you can borrow based on your cost of attendance and other financial aid you receive. You are responsible for paying the interest on a direct unsubsidized loan during all periods. If you choose not to pay the interest while you are in school and during grace periods and deferment or forbearance periods, your interest will accrue (accumulate) and be capitalized (that is, your interest will be added to the principal amount of your loan).

3. **Direct PLUS Loans** are loans made to graduate or professional students and **parents** of dependent undergraduate students to help pay for education expenses not covered by other financial aid. The US Department of Education is the lender. The borrower must not have an adverse credit history, and the maximum loan amount is the student's cost of attendance (determined by the school) minus any other financial aid received.

4. **Direct Consolidation Loans** allow you to combine all of your eligible federal student loans into a single loan with a single loan servicer.

I'd like to take a moment to address a serious issue with regard to borrowing money to pay for college. One day, while driving to work, I tuned in to a certain radio station. Lo and behold, the commentators were discussing the most recent *US News and World Report's* "Best Colleges" ranking. The argument was, should a student borrow up to $200,000 to attend one of the best colleges in America? Their answer was no because they felt that a student could get a quality education by attending a local community college or the state's public college. Their reasoning was that it doesn't make sense to attend a great college or university because of a magazine's ranking of universities.

I had to really think about what they were saying. I asked myself why a student would attend Stanford or Princeton University and come away not being able to find a job and up to her eyeballs with a $200,000 loan balance? The answer is simple. It's the same reason why you come out of a grocery store with more stuff than you originally went there for. Either you had a plan and didn't stick to it or you got distracted and carried away. Many students get accepted to college and have no clue of what they should be doing with that $200,000 education they are receiving. It's as simple as that. In fact, 73 percent of parents have no plan for college, and I am willing to go out on a limb and say that 73 percent of students attending college have no idea what they are going to do upon graduation. I say that because according to a CBS News survey of 2,134 workers, only 47 percent reported to be working in their fields of study. This means that fewer than half of the students surveyed were working anywhere close to what they attended college for. The survey also showed that 32 percent of college graduates reported never working in the field of their major. I will expound on this later in the book, but it's something to keep in mind when thinking about borrowing money for college.

The **Federal Perkins Loan Program** is a school-based loan program for undergraduates and graduate students with exceptional financial need. These are low-interest loans, but not all schools participate in the program. You'll want to check with your school's financial-aid office to see if your school participates. With a Perkins loan, your school is the lender; you will make your payments either to the school that made your loan or to your school's loan servicer. The amount of funds you receive will depend on your financial need and the availability of funds at your college.

Federal grants: Remember, grants are sought after because they are free money—financial aid that doesn't have to be repaid. Grants are often *need-based*, while scholarships are usually *merit-based*. The US Department of Education offers a variety of federal grants to students attending four-year colleges or universities, community colleges, and career schools.

The **Federal Pell Grant** is the best-known grant. It's usually awarded only to undergraduate students who have not earned a bachelor's or a professional degree. The amounts of the grant can change yearly. The Department of Education listed the maximum Federal Pell Grant award as $5,645 for the 2013–14 award year (July 1, 2013, to June 30, 2014). For the 2014–15 award year (July 1, 2014, to June 30,

2015), the maximum award will be $5,730. The amount you get, though, will depend on the following:

- Your financial need
- Your cost of attendance
- Your status as a full-time or part-time student
- Your plans to attend school for a full academic year or less

If you're eligible for a federal Pell Grant, you'll receive the full amount you qualify for because each school participating in the program receives enough funds each year from the government to pay the Federal Pell Grant amounts for all of its eligible students. The amount of any other student aid you might qualify for does not affect the amount of your Federal Pell Grant.

A **Federal Supplemental Educational Opportunity Grant** (FSEOG) is a grant for undergraduate students with exceptional financial need. Students who will receive Pell grants and have the most financial need will receive FSEOGs first. The FSEOG program is administered directly by the financial-aid office at each participating school and is therefore called "campus-based" aid. Check with your school to find out if it offers the FSEOG because not all schools do.

You can receive between $100 and $4,000 a year, depending on your financial need, when you apply, the amount of other aid you get, and the availability of funds at your school. Each participating school receives a certain amount of FSEOG funds each year from the US Department of Education's office of Federal Student Aid. Once the full amount of the school's FSEOG funds has been awarded to students, no more FSEOG awards can be made for that year. This system works differently from the Pell grant program, which provides funds to every eligible student. Your best bet for qualifying for this grant is to make sure you apply for federal student aid as early as you can. Each school sets its own deadlines for campus-based funds, so ask what those deadlines are.

The **Teacher Education Assistance for College and Higher Education (TEACH)** grant is not for everyone, but if your child is thinking about becoming a teacher, this source of funds is worth considering. A TEACH grant can help you pay for college if you plan to become a teacher in a high-need field in a low-income area. You'll be required to teach for a certain length of time, so make sure you understand your obligation. A TEACH grant is different from other federal student grants because it requires you to take certain kinds of classes to get the grant and then do a certain kind of job to keep the grant from turning into a loan.

Iraq and Afghanistan Service Grants: If a student's parent or guardian died as a result of military service in Iraq or Afghanistan, he or she may be eligible for an Iraq and Afghanistan Service Grant. Like other federal grants, Iraq and Afghanistan Service Grants provide money to college or career school students to help pay their education expenses.

College Work–Study: It's not exactly a grant, but the Federal Work–Study program provides part-time jobs for undergraduate and graduate students with financial need, allowing them to earn money to help pay education expenses. The program encourages community service work and work related to the student's course of study.

State and local governments: Even if you're not eligible for federal aid, you might be eligible for financial aid from your state. Some states have better programs or more programs than others. Some of them have special programs for people who want to be teachers or health professionals or for minority groups. The best way to find out about these state programs is to contact the State Higher Education Agency and have them send you information about the different programs. You can also go to ed.gov and view the Education Resource Organization Directory. It provides information on grants, scholarships, and other financial aid for college students from the states, including federal-supported state programs such as Byrd scholarships and LEAP (Leveraging Educational Assistance Partnership) grants. If your child is potentially a candidate for any of them, you'll definitely want to take advantage of the opportunity and apply.

Collegiate Resources

Colleges are a major source of free money. Many colleges offer financial aid from their own funds, usually from their endowments. This is money donated by alumni or from sources outside of the federal and state governments. A lot of people are confused about endowments and how they work. They tend to think it's just a huge pool of money the school can dip into anytime it wants. But Albert Phung, a writer and analyst for Investopedia.com, offered this clear explanation in one of his investment articles:

> Endowments represent money or other financial assets that are donated to universities or colleges. The sole intention of the endowment is to invest it, so that the total asset value will yield an inflation-adjusted principal amount, along with additional income for further

investments and supplementary expenditures. Typically, endowment funds follow a fairly strict policy allocation, which is a set of long-term guidelines that dictates the asset allocation that will yield the targeted return requirement without taking on too much risk.

Most endowments have guidelines that state how much of each year's investment income can be spent. For many universities, this amount is about 5 percent of the endowment's total asset value. Because some of the more coveted schools, such as Harvard, have endowments worth billions of dollars, this 5 percent can equal a large sum of money.

Endowment donors can sometimes restrict schools on how they can spend this money. For example, donors can decide to use a portion of an endowment's scheduled income on a merit-based or need-based scholarship. Another standard restrictive use of an endowment's income is to provide funding for endowed professorships, which are used to attract world-class educators.

Other than these restrictions, universities can use the rest of the allotted spending amount as standard income. Decisions about whether it should be spent on hiring professors, upgrading/repairing facilities, or funding more scholarships is left up to school administrators. An endowment's investment income can also significantly lower tuition costs for students. For example, if a university's endowment yields a total of

$150 million and has a 5 percent spending limit, this would provide $7.5 million of available income. If the university had originally budgeted $5.5 million in endowment funds, this would mean that the excess $2 million could be used to pay other debts/expenses—savings that could be passed on to students.

However, because universities depend on investment returns for supplementary income, there could be trouble if the investments do not yield a suitable amount of returns. Therefore, most endowments are run by professionals to ensure that the investments made are in line with the aforementioned policy allocation.

So the schools do have this sizable source of funds, and that's good because at a private school you'll need it. Remember, you have a much bigger gap to fill because it's more expensive to attend a private school. You're also going to find that this type of funding is awarded on a first-come, first-served basis. If you wait to apply until the very last minute, which unfortunately a lot of parents do, you will miss out on a lot of this money because they give preference to people who get their forms in the earliest. Once their source of free money is gone, it's pretty much gone. The school has met its budget for the year.

The other thing that you should be looking at is where your child fits in the academic standing of the schools he is considering. If he is applying to, let's say, a middle-range college and he falls in the top 25 percent of the average of applicants based on his grade point average and SAT or ACT scores, that's a good thing. That means he has a good shot at getting what's called "preferential packaging," a financial-aid package more heavily weighted with free money and fewer loans. Schools obviously want to attract better students with better packages. If you're not a good student or don't have the greatest grades and scores, the school may fill your need, but they'll do it with more loans and less grant money.

Many times, students will apply to college and receive no free money. That's when I tell them, "You didn't fall within the top twenty-five percent." Understanding the statistics of who gets accepted at these colleges and who's going to get the free money is critical. Knowing where you fit in and who would really want you is a must because that's who's going to give you the most money. Once you know that, you'll have a better shot of getting the free money from a particular school.

Private Sources

Many organizations offer scholarships or grants to help students pay for college. These are the Coca-Cola scholarships, the Shriner scholarships, and the Burger King scholarships. This is the resource most people understand the least, and they get extremely excited over the idea of getting a private scholarship that's going to pay for everything because their kid plays volleyball with her left pinky and she's one-quarter Native American, and she is from a certain tribe. In no way, shape, or fashion am I belittling Native Americans, because my grandmother was one-sixteenth Cherokee.

Very, very rarely do people get these types of funds. Yes, they do exist. Yes, some people get them. I personally would say that if you want to spend any time on this search, go after the local private awards that you can find from your local guidance office. Just ask them what they have in the community from insurance companies or from certain publishing companies that are local.

Remember the 3 percent figure from our list above? Here's the thing about this small piece of the financial-aid pie. These scholarships are usually nonrenewable, which means you'll receive them only once. It's highly unlikely to see scholarships that are renewed for four years. Some are out there, but they're very hard to get. If you do land one of these scholarships, a lot of people think it's a great thing—that this free money can make a real difference in how affordable your child's education is.

But here's the thing: A lot of colleges will count that scholarship against you as income. Let's say, for example, that your cost of attendance is $30,000 at whatever college, your need is $20,000, and you receive a $5,000 scholarship. The $5,000 will automatically knock your need down to $15,000. At this point, you'd get $15,000 from the school and $5,000 from the scholarship to meet your need. However, there's still a difference of $10,000! Why can't the college simply meet your $20,000 in need and allow your child to keep the extra $5,000 that he worked so hard for? That would bring your out-of-pocket cost down to $5,000.

And think about this: You're going to get that scholarship only once, right? It's only for one year. What happens next year? The cost of the college goes up. Without additional outside scholarships, your need increases. In most cases, this means one thing: you're pretty much stuck. A word of caution: don't spend your time looking for crumbs. What does that mean? That's where we go back again to the 3 percent figure. If you plan on spending 96.8 percent of your time going after these scholarships, which represent only 3 percent of the pie, you're wasting a lot of time, energy, and money going after crumbs.

Think about what you have to do to have a chance to win this morsel. This is what I truly feel families should do. Instead of wasting time applying for scholarships, a better idea is to have the student work to raise his or her GPA, SAT, and ACT scores. The higher marks will help you obtain more free money for four years. Usually, merit-based aid from the college is allotted over a four-year period of time, not for just the first year, not just the second year or third, but for four years. So the higher the student's SAT score, ACT score, and GPA, the taller she stands among the other candidates.

So it is wise to have your children to spend their time investing in their scores and grades versus looking for free money. Also, I recommend that parents not pay for private scholarship search services because at best, they are hit and miss. You need something solid.

CHAPTER 4

How to Apply for Aid

Before you start down the road of applying for financial aid, I'm going to set up some flares and draw your attention to my big *warning* sign, which I've conveniently posted for your benefit. What's the deal with this sign? It's there because I want to have your complete focus when I say this one thing, and it's hugely important:

 You have one shot at getting it right.

That means you have one shot at filing for financial aid in such a way that you get optimum results. Why? Because the first year of college is the most important one in terms of your negotiating power. It's the one time schools will be in competition to attract you. Once the student matriculates, they know they have you, and they know your child's preference will be to stay there. They won't be as pliable when it comes to wrangling for more aid the following years. So your best chance at scoring the most free money for as long as possible will be in the first year. And it will be based on what you do in the first application process.

If something goes wrong when you initially apply for aid, you'll suffer the effects for far longer than you realize. Let's say you apply for college and financial aid without preparing for the process. I'm going to assume the following. Number one, you've waited until the last minute. Number two, you've gotten information from the wrong people. You've applied and received absolutely nothing! You inquire and soon discover that a bunch of ill-advised mistakes were made on the forms. You frantically call the school and explain the situation. They say, "Please calm down. These are all simple mistakes that can be fixed. They're all verifiable. It's just honest stuff. Complete our verification forms, and we'll see what can be done." The school checks it out, but by the time the fixing process is over, they can only tell you, "We're out of money for the year. Better luck next year."

Well, when you come back next year, here's what happens. You're going to apply for financial aid again. But if your child attends a school that has a bad history of giving out financial-aid packages in a student's second year, you're pretty much done—game over. Here's why: Colleges know and understand that you and your child have gone through hell getting them acclimated to college that first year. You've shed all your tears. You've gotten used to her not being there. She has gotten used to not being at home. She has gained some independence, and she has tasted freedom! Some colleges will take advantage of all that, which means you may see a dip in your financial aid. Why? Because they know you're probably not going to want to take your child away from college, especially if she has done well and you want to keep that going. You will find everything under any rock to keep your child in school, and it's going to cost you more money.

That's why, to avoid this squeeze, you've got to do the financial-aid process right the first time. Besides, once your child moves back home, it can take years just to get her back out of your house! I don't know of any parent who wants to relive the teenage years but with an adult. According to a survey completed by Robi Ludwig, PsyD, and Coldwell Banker, in which they gathered information on more than two thousand people, most people disagree over how long is too long for college graduates to live with their parents. Millennials (ages eighteen to thirty-four) think it's acceptable to live at home with their parents for as long as five years after college. Older Americans (defined as age fifty-five and older for the purpose of the survey) disagree, believing these young adults, if they do move back home after school, should move out within three years of graduating.

FAFSA: The Form of All Forms

The first thing you have to do to apply for financial aid is complete the Free Application for Federal Student Aid (FAF-SA) form. This is the federal form every single school that offers any type of federal funding will require you to fill out. Everyone has to fill it out to get financial aid, and you can't apply for federal loans if you don't fill one out. A lot of people say, "Oh, it's just a form, it's no big deal." Believe it or not, a large percentage of FAFSA forms are submitted with errors or inconsistencies. And simple actions can mess up this form, whether you complete it online or on paper. You're not sup-posed to use correction fluid when you make corrections on the hard copy. If you omit a Social Security number or forget to sign the form, details like that can bump a form.

If the form gets bumped, it takes another four to six weeks to reprocess it. That's a really long time in the world of finan-cial aid. Remember, aid gets awarded on a first-come, first-served basis. You don't want your FAFSA getting bumped be-cause it will result in your receiving less aid—in many cases, thousands of dollars less just because of a simple error. So you want to make sure that the form is not only filled out, but filled out properly.

Allow me to share with you one example of an error. I'll be honest and tell you that this is one of the biggest undetected errors you can make on your financial-aid forms! Let's assume you have $405,000.00 in your 401(k) account. Quick question: Is your 401(k) account an investment? Yes, it is, but for FAFSA purposes, the answer is no. However, I've seen many people include their 401(k)s and other employer-sponsored retirement plans with their regular investments.

A Word about Timing

Some colleges are going back as many as two years to see if you made any financial moves to improve your situation for financial aid. When people ask me, "When should we start preparing?" I always advise them to start during your child's freshman or sophomore year of high school. That's when you should begin preparing and positioning yourself to start the process of completing financial-aid forms. You'll want to take a good look at your financial picture and consider what needs to be done. Once you figure that out, you'll then need to seek out the best experts to help you do it. I mentioned earlier that following the wrong advice is a huge mistake that many people make. Remember, the best advice isn't always free. The other problem with getting the wrong advice is this: often you don't know it's wrong until it's too late to be corrected.

If you're reading this book, you probably don't think this way. On the other hand, you may be someone who does. I'm simply sharing this because these are the very families who need the most help with the situation but just don't realize it. I say this because I often get the following question, "Harold, what if I don't know if my student is going to college?" I think they ask this because they are simply afraid of the process and just don't know where to turn.

On another timing issue, I should point out that there's a notation on the FAFSA form that says, "Get an estimate out before February 15th, but don't wait until April." What does that mean? This is an instruction for people who think, "Well, I've got to have my taxes done before I can fill out my financial-aid forms." But that's not correct. You just need to estimate your income for that year.

For example, as of this writing, we're in the 2014–15 school year. Let's say you're going to fill out your FAFSA in January 2015 for the 2015–16 school year. Most people don't have their taxes done until March or April. Some will even file after April, but you really don't want to wait that long to file your FAFSA. You have to fill out your FAFSA form and just estimate your income. If you're filing online, simply click the "estimate" button. The form goes in, and the schools will get all your information and begin to work on your application. Later they will ask you to update your taxes after you've filed them. However, your estimate must be accurate because if you get awarded financial aid based on that estimate and it varies drastically from the actual figure, they're going to pull that financial aid away from you.

The CSS Form: A Puzzle to Piece Together

The next major form you have to complete is the College Board's CSS/Financial Aid PROFILE form. The CSS PROFILE is the form the private schools want. All schools use the FAFSA, and then a handful of schools rely on the CSS PROFILE. This has always been a difficult form to navigate, but recently the College Board made it even more complicated. Now, not only is the PROFILE an additional form, but you have to register to become a CSS member, *then* you have to register for the actual PROFILE form! Also, you can only register and fill out the application online. The College Board will not accept any paper versions of the registration or application.

So the first thing you have to do is go to the College Board's website (www.collegeboard.com) and search to see if any of the schools you are applying to are listed as using the CSS/ Financial Aid PROFILE. It will tell you every single one of the schools that will request the form for the current academic year. You'll want to make sure you're looking at the current year because here's the thing about the PROFILE schools: in some years, a school will be a PROFILE school and in other years, it will not be a PROFILE school—it will drop out of the program. There's no clear explanation of this. It may depend on the school's funding, how its endowment is doing, or what its previous experience as a PROFILE school has been.

If your schools are listed, then the next step is to sign up to become a collegeboard.com member (signup is free). Once you are a member, then you can register for the PROFILE form. Make sure to have your credit card available; there is a nominal fee for the PROFILE form registration and for *each* school you will be listing.

Once you've become a College Board member and registered to get the PROFILE, you then fill out and complete your PROFILE form. This form used to be only a standard form, but the College Board now allows each private school to add to the core questions any of the about two hundred additional "optional" questions that each institution can choose from. For example, Harvard has a supplement to the CSS profile. As of this writing, Yale has a supplement to the CSS profile, as do some religious schools.

These additional questions will appear in Section Q of the PROFILE form. So if you're applying to five or six schools that want a PROFILE, you could end up with five different schools that want a whole lot of different questions in addition to the core questions. The private schools request these additional questions because they want more detailed information to help them figure out your financial picture. Remember, they have a lot at stake as far as giving out money. They want to make sure they're giving in the right places.

The additional questions usually ask about home equity and a more detailed explanation of your income, assets, and expenses. Religious schools will ask what parish you worship at and what your involvement in that particular church is like. Some schools will ask you about your real estate and other assets like your car. I know one school that would send out a supplement asking how many cars you own and when you bought them. Why? Because they know some people will try to follow the advice out there, which says that if you have a lot of extra money in your accounts, before you fill out your FAF-SA, you should pay off your bills, pay off all your credit card debt, and go buy new cars. That way, you essentially hide the money from the forms. But when a school comes back and asks you these extra questions, they'll see that you recently bought cars and so on and so forth, unless you choose to lie. We'll get into the lying piece in a later chapter.

They're asking for cash flow in these supplemental questions. It is very, very interesting that a college would want to know your personal finances at such an in-depth level when you probably don't even know yourself! They do it because they're really looking for whether or not you're as indigent as you claim to be on your financial-aid forms. They can determine all of that.

Your answers must be consistent with the Free Application for Federal Student Aid (FAFSA). If you have discrepancies, they will ask you a lot of additional questions. And I can assure you, it's not easy to resolve these discrepancies. A lot of people think it's easy, but again, there's plenty of room for error. The schools look at these things with a fine-tooth comb, so you want to make sure that you do them right. If you don't, you're going to get less aid.

Yet Another Set of Forms: The School's Own

After filling out the FAFSA and the CSS PROFILE, the next roadblock in the maze of things they require you to do to get aid is to fill out the school's own institutional forms. Most schools are going to ask you the same questions you answered in the previous forms, but they will ask them in a different way. It's kind of like an audit. They'll call it the "income verification worksheet" or "asset verification worksheet" due to the fact that something you said on the PROFILE or something you said on the FAFSA just doesn't add up. They're going to need you to state that again on another form so they can come to an accurate conclusion. Again, this form has to be consistent with the other two forms or else it will generate a lot of questions. So if you screw one up, you've got to screw them all up in the same place. That way, they know you're not really trying to cheat them out of any money. On a positive note, these forms are a little bit easier than the others, and these forms aren't likely to get bumped because you're sending them directly to the school rather than to a federal processing agency.

The Business/Farm Supplement Form

If you own a business or a farm, colleges often ask for separate documentation on those finances because businesses tend to have different ways of shielding certain assets. A lot of people think farmers don't make a lot of money. Sometimes they can make a lot, but in most cases, the land they own is the biggest asset. The interesting thing about the business form is that you almost need to send it to your CPA because they're going to ask you about your business's book value. They're going to ask you a lot of terms that you may not be familiar with because they really want to see if there's any money left in the company that maybe you should've taken in the form of a distribution or draw, or maybe you could've taken that as a salary, paid taxes, and used the funds for college. I own a business, and I've had to complete these forms every single year for the PROFILE. It's not an easy form. It's extremely complicated, and you have to be very careful about what you put on that form.

The Divorced/Separated Agreement Form

If you're divorced or separated, the school could try to hunt down your ex to see what they have to pay for college. In one example, we had a client who was divorced. The husband remarried and moved away. His agreement with her was, "I'll pay child support, nothing more. I'm not going to help you with college." That was actually written into the divorce decree. But the university the student attended said, "No, we couldn't care less. We want to see what this gentleman has in income, and we want to see what he has in assets."

We found out where the father lived, got his information, and sent it over to the school. As a result, the EFC increased drastically to a tremendous amount of money.

We had to appeal and let the school know that this was not the mom's fault. Her ex was *not* willing to pay. They came back and said, "We know it's not her fault, but just because he doesn't want to pay and doesn't want to fulfill his responsibility doesn't mean we should automatically let him off the hook."

I said, "You're right, you shouldn't. But you're hurting her because he's not going to pay. You're forcing her EFC up, and she's not able to pay it. Therefore, her son is not going to be able to continue to attend college." They were asking her to pay $60,000 at that school, and it was unfair. She had no legal recourse. Paying college tuition is not like having to pay child support, in which case you can go to court and have a judge say, "You're a deadbeat dad. We're going to throw you in jail for not paying for college." The law just doesn't reach that far. In some extreme cases, I wish it did, but it doesn't. Eventually we convinced the school to reverse its decision. The EFC was lowered to an amount that made her son's education affordable. Hats off to that university!

This type of case is becoming all too familiar. One of my objectives in writing this book is to give you a sense of the problems you'll face with various forms as you begin the financial-aid process. The colleges want to see you jump through about thirty different hoops before they give you money and they do this, in my opinion, on purpose because a lot of people drop out in frustration and don't get aid. That's why you've got to have patience, take control, and understand the system if you want to get all you're eligible for.

Do You Cheat?

I deliberated about this section a quite a bit. And to be honest, I almost didn't include it in the book. The reason is that if you're reading this book, you are looking for legitimate ways to get your children through college. Cheating is probably the furthest thing from your mind. So before you proceed, here's a word of caution: I wrote this section for informational purposes only. I wanted to give you a glimpse into the thought process and the outcomes for people who feel that cheating may be an option. It is not an assessment or assassination of your character or belief system.

First, I want to address some of the common types of fraud.

Common Types of Fraud

The most common types of fraud involve underreporting of income and assets and overstating the number of family members in college. Some families may even go so far as to provide a falsified copy of their income tax returns.

Financial-aid offices are advised to look for the following warning signs[2]:

- Interest and dividend income both zero or very low when compared with the family's wages. Compare these figures with any figures reported for capital gains or losses.
- No alimony income reported or alimony payments reported when the custodial parent is female
- No business or farm income reported when the parents' occupation suggests that they are self-employed.

---

2   "FAA Guide to Detecting Fraud on Financial Adi Applications,"
    FinAid website, http://www.finaid.org/educators/fraud.phtml).

    If the return reports one-half of self-employment tax or
self-employed health insurance deduction but no business or farm income, be suspicious.

- Check the return for the telltale signs that it is a photocopy of a photocopy. If it appears to be a photocopy of
an original, be suspicious.
- Round numbers like $0, $500, and $1,000 used
for income

I'd also like to point out that colleges also have programs
in place that help them combat this issue.

I first asked myself, "Why would a person even want to
consider cheating as an option?" The answer that came to
me was quite simple. Many people look at what it takes to
pay for college and see a very intimidating and daunting task.
Unfortunately, their view is far from inaccurate. The cost of
a college education can cost anywhere from $70,000 to
$200,000 or as much as a million dollars, depending on the
number of children you have, how many years they spend in
school, where they go to college, and what they study.

The sad truth is, many families don't plan. As a matter of
fact, they fail to plan and even worse, their plan fails! So the
only option many people feel they have is to cheat. I know it's
not the right thing to do, but there is a lot of information out
there on how to reposition their situation illegally. Some people use complicated schemes, yet some of their tactics are
simple. Some just flat-out lie when they fill out the financial-
aid forms. Let me give you some examples.

In one case, a family came to me and said, "OK, I own
this property. But I heard I could give the property to a family
member during the time my student is in college and then

once the process is all done, my family member can give it back to me. Is that legal?" Giving property to your family is legal. However, is it legal to give them property so that you can get it out of your asset base when applying for financial aid? This is a very slippery slope. Why?

When you gift assets, either cash or real property, the IRS sets a specific limit. You can find detailed information regarding gifting on the IRS's website at http://www.irs.gov/Businesses/Small-Businesses-%26-Self-Employed/Frequently-Asked-Questions-on-Gift-Taxes#2. On this website, you can see that a lot goes into gifting property, and there are many different requirements to meet.

Giving away property can raise several questions. Let's assume you give property to a family member with the agreement that as soon as college is done or at some date in the future, they're supposed to give it back to you. The transaction is executed. You apply for financial aid but don't receive it. You are now stuck in the position of not having access to the property so that you can get equity out of it to pay your out-of-pocket cost. You're also out the legal fees it cost you to set this up and then tear it back down because it didn't work. Many other issues can arise from this transaction as well. So before venturing out into these types of strategies, consider all of the potential disasters.

In another situation, I had someone say, "We have all of this cash in our accounts, and to get rid of it, I'll transfer it to my family member's bank account. He doesn't have any children, so this shouldn't affect him at all."

I asked the following two questions. Number one, what's preventing that family member from going to Las Vegas and gambling it away? Number two, and this is the worst situation: what if the family member passes away and is married? Wouldn't his spouse and children (if he had any) be entitled to the money? What if his spouse had no idea where the money came from and now has to take your word for it that it belongs to you? I'm not convinced that's the way to go.

There are many other issues that could arise, too. In the worst situation of cheating, I have heard of people creating separate tax returns—one prepared and filed with the IRS, and another prepared and used to show income for financial aid. This practice was commonplace until the IRS gave colleges a powerful tool to help combat the efforts of cheaters. It's the IRS Data Retrieval Tool. With this tool, colleges can have a copy of the tax return that the applicant filed with the IRS downloaded directly to them! Talk about high-tech!

This tool links your taxes to your FAFSA application, and it pulls everything over into the FAFSA automatically. There's no way you can cheat unless you file a fraudulent tax return. Of course, if you file a fraudulent tax return, then you have to deal with the IRS. However, this won't stop everyone from trying to game the system. Some people may not put down all of the income they earn, and they file that tax return. Yes, they'll save on taxes. Yes, they'll get financial aid.   T h e n they go back and amend the tax return, saying, "We made a mistake." They simply pay the extra taxes to the IRS. But here's what you don't know: the college can audit you, too. You could become part of a college's audit process where they say, "Let's see if anyone changed their tax returns. Let's go back and look at all of the tax returns." They might take a sample of, say, three thousand FAFSAs they received that year and audit them. If you went in and made adjustments to your tax return after you were awarded financial aid, then you could have to pay back all of the aid you received. If they see that you did it fraudulently, then they impose a $10,000 fine or a year in jail or both, depending on what you did.

In another instance, I've heard of spouses claiming that they were divorced and filing separate tax returns. The FAFSA was filed with the parent who had the lowest income.

I've had a number of people say, "We'll take all of our cash and stick it in a safe and then not report it on the FAFSA. How are they going to know?" Let me remind you that on the FAFSA is a question regarding cash. It's not asking about cash only in the bank, it's asking about cash, period. You have $300,000 sitting in a safe and you're going to ask for financial aid?

Unfortunately, it's not uncommon to see this. Someone asked the question, "What if we take all of our assets and pay off our house? We have this much in the bank. We owe this much on our mortgage. What if we just paid off our bills and got rid of the cash?" There's a ton of incorrect information on the Internet recommending strategies like this. Some so-called experts suggest that instead of paying for college, you should go buy new cars, pay off all your credit card debt, and get rid of all your cash—by paying off the mortgage, for example.

Some colleges will take your home equity into consideration on the financial-aid form, and some colleges will not. It depends on the type of college you're applying to, including whether it's a private school or a profile school. (Remember: A profile school uses the CSS profile form in addition to the FAFSA. You can look up profile schools at cssprofile.com. The CSS Profile Form will ask much more in-depth questions regarding your financial situation. It will ask about home equity,

401(k) accounts, and basically any type of asset that you may have, such as trust accounts and so on and so forth.)

Some people own businesses, and sometimes they tend to fudge numbers. Colleges are a little savvier than they used to be. They now have far more tools at their disposal. One of those tools is the IDOC (Institutional Documentation) service form from the College Board. Some private colleges and universities require you to submit this form. One of the forms included in this packet is the Business/Farm Supplement. If you own a business, it must be completed. This form is extremely specific.

When It's an Attitude Thing

As with any form of cheating, the mindset of the people who cheat plays a big role in the process. Many people who think about cheating may feel a sense of entitlement. Because they pay taxes into the system and the schools are federally funded, isn't a portion of the financial-aid pool rightfully theirs in the first place? I would say yes. However, this isn't a good reason for not following the rules of the game. There are many other ways to get your fair share. Some people say, "Well, they're not going to catch everybody." That is correct. Not everyone is going to get caught. However, a handful of families are being caught. Do you really want to take that risk?

The people who try to cheat throughout this process usually don't have good moral character anyway. Because of that, schools have made it extremely difficult on everyone just because of the cheaters who are in the system.

Here's an example:

Some foreigners will come to our country and try to take

advantage of the system. Because of that, the US government is starting to crack down. These individuals have money in their home countries, but then they move to the United States and feign poverty. "We don't have anything," they say, but one thing I've noticed is that they have really smart children. When I come across these types of situations and the numbers don't add up, I ask the following: "How is it that you make fifty thousand dollars a year and you own a condominium worth half a million dollars? How did you obtain the money to purchase it? Was it a gift? What exactly was or is the situation?" In this situation, there are too many unanswered questions, and I really don't intend to get too personal or make the family feel too uncomfortable. My objective is to see how I can help them. It bothers me because their children are in tutoring and other various activities, and I simply wonder how they are paying for all of this because I don't see very much income or assets on paper. As mentioned earlier, this book was written for families who fall within the middle and upper-middle class because they have the toughest time paying for college, and these are just a few examples why.

As a planner, I believe this is a complicated situation that is best left to be handled by the experts. As a result of this type of activity, our government created new laws that are aimed to help curtail the problem. A lot of money is given out to people who are not forthcoming, and this makes it extremely difficult for college administrations. When you cheat, you may gain some short-term benefits, but please keep in mind that many people are hurt because of this.

And you damage your own family, substantially so, when you cheat. It's vitally important for you to understand that.

I wrote this book because I want you to know you don't

have to do this. There are better ways of getting your children through college that are perfectly moral and legal. But the key is starting early. I share with parents that the best thing to do is get it correct from the very beginning. Here's how. Sit down with your children at an early age and talk about this subject of going to college. Keep talking about it. And please sit down with a professional and create a plan of action. Also, be proactive in updating that plan along the way.

Unfortunately a lot of people come to me with the mistaken notion that I can help them cheat because I put a lot of emphasis on improving their chances for getting financial aid. People often ask where they should hide a particular asset. I let them know that seeking answers to those types of questions is truly unacceptable. What I can do is this: I can put together a long-term financial plan to satisfy their college funding requirements. As a planner, if you're reading this book, it is totally unprofessional—and illegal, might I add—to give advice that puts a family at risk for being suspected of cheating to get financial aid. Any person who hires you should have a plan created that meets all of his or her long-term financial responsibilities. Anything less than that is a huge disservice. It also casts a negative light on honest legitimate planners. What's worse is that if your advice harms a family, they will probably never seek help again.

Here's an idea of what a great plan looks like:

It has to get all students through college in four years in a comfortable manner.

Number two, it has to pay off all of the client's debts prior to retirement or put them in a position where they have this option. Number three, it also has to show that their assets are going to be passed on through estate planning with little to no tax. Number four, the plan has to be guaranteed to work with NO RISK! Let me repeat that. NO RISK! Bottom line, it's a long-term picture. When I speak with a prospective client, I ask questions such as, "What's your long-term plan to get through four years of college?" "Where does that leave you for retirement?" Eventually the question becomes, "Do you feel you now need a long-term plan that will cover college, your lifestyle, your retirement, your estate planning and all of that?" If the answer is "Yes, we need a plan, we want you to do that for us, we want it long-term," then they're a good fit for our firm.

If they come in and say, "Oh no, we're just looking for something for the next four years. We just need to get through these next four years and that's it," I have to decline. There's a lot of work that goes into positioning a family to get their students through college and then the next 30 or 40 years of their life. If they're not interested in that, I shouldn't take them on as clients.

The majority of the financial planners who are in this line of work think the same way, and they're pretty much up to par. If you do find one that's not being honest and they sell strategies that hide your assets, that's when you want to run because those strategies, even if they are legal, don't last for long. A lot of so-called planners have taken advantage of people. They've used the profession as a get rich quick scheme to scam people for scholarships and to make a quick buck. Many parents are at their wits end trying to figure out what to do. They're at a very vulnerable time, so they can easily be taken advantage of. If you don't have a financial planner and you don't know who to talk to and you don't know where to turn, you could fall prey to that.

CHAPTER 5

The Award Letter and Leveraging for Aid

Most readers will see the word "leverage" in the title of this chapter and assume they will learn here how to wield some sort of influence to help their family obtain more financial aid. After all, the word "leverage" is synonymous with words such as "control," "power," "force," "pull," and "clout." And you would think that because the family is the paying customer, it would have some sort of influence or clout in this expensive transaction that's about to be made. But that's not the case. Here's what you need to know about financial-aid leveraging: the colleges are the ones doing the leveraging, not necessarily the parents. When it comes to financial aid, leveraging is the process universities use to determine the smallest amount of financial aid they can award to a particular student and still get that student to enroll.

Roughly 65 percent of private schools and 27 percent of public schools engage in financial-aid leveraging. The private schools do it at a much higher rate because, of course, they have bigger endowments and therefore have more free money to give away. Public universities, as stated earlier in this book, are state and federally funded, and their endowment funds are minuscule compared to that of a private school, especially one with big-time donors.

Here's how the leveraging works. Let's say your child gets

accepted to Xavier University. Your cost of attendance at Xavier will depend on whether your child is an in-state student or out-of-state student. But for now let's say, hypothetically, your cost of attendance is $40,000 a year. You went through the financial-aid process. You filled out the various forms, the FAFSA form, the CSS PROFILE, etc., and it was determined that your family contribution was $20,000. So $40,000 minus $20,000 equals $20,000.

I know right off the bat that at Xavier University, you are eligible for $20,000 worth of financial aid based only on financial need. If the administrators at Xavier wanted to leverage the situation, they would say, "OK, does this student really want to come to this school?" They will review the student's files and see where else the student applied for college. If Xavier is the best school on that list, it kind likely means that the student wants to go to that university no matter what.

Once they have this information, the school will say, "We know this family qualifies for $20,000, but let's see what happens if we offer them $10,000. Will the student still come to this school if we offer $10,000 less than their need?" This happens quite a bit.

The point is, you'll want to keep this leveraging business in mind once you have a financial-aid award letter in your hands. The offer may not be what you want it to be, but the numbers, as permanent as they might look, are not written in stone. How do you analyze the award letter, taking into account that the college might engage in leveraging? What does a quality offer look like? Let's look at some examples of financial-aid award letters. I've graded them for you, but we'll also look at the details that cause the offer to be a strong or weak one.

Analyzing Award Letters

University 1

This award letter is for the 2013 14 school year and, for the family involved, this was an out-of-state school. Let's start with this important point: the student is in his junior year of college. That fact will already make this a very different award letter than one received by an incoming freshman. The family filed its FAFSA, and the number that the federal government said they could pay—their expected family contribution—was $7,051. That's all they could see the family was able to pay. The student's contribution was $140.

The college looked at the information and basically said, "We're going to give this student, who is a junior in college, a tuition/need grant of $4,500, a subsidized Federal Direct Loan of $5,500, an unsubsidized Federal Direct Loan for $2,000, and a tuition grant scholarship for $2,000." Now, let's break down each piece of this offer.

- The **first grant** is based on need. That's free money the family doesn't have to pay back.
- The **subsidized Federal Direct Loan** is a loan from the federal government. It's based on what year the student is in school. It's also based on need because if you don't have a need for financial aid, in most cases, you can't get the subsidized loan from the federal government.
- The **unsubsidized Federal Direct Loan** is one the family will have to pay the interest on as it accumulates while the student is in school.
- The **tuition grant scholarship** is a basic merit-based

grant offered by that particular school.

So altogether, the college awarded this family $14,000 for the student's junior year. This is very interesting. The federal government said the max this family could afford to pay was $7,051 a year. The cost of this college is about $42,000 per year, so that means this family has a need of$35,000. But the university took it upon itself to say, "We're not going to give them that. We're going to give them only $14,000." Let's do the math: $42,000 minus $14,000 is $28,000. The family can afford to pay only $7,051. They were left short four times what they can afford to pay in this student's junior year.

I found this appalling. But it also shows the vital importance of this fact: colleges give away the most free money in the student's first year. That's why I share with parents of incoming freshman that you have only *one* shot at going through the process correctly and gaining the right award. Over the course of student's college career, some schools will tend to reduce the amount of financial aid because they know they've "got you." The child is about to graduate, so *Boom!* You get hit with this big bill out of the blue in your student's junior year. I know this scenario may sound a little dramatic, but I need your attention for what I'm about to say. At the really good schools, you will *rarely* have this problem. That's why it is critical to pick the right school from the beginning.

However, when this happens to a family, they usually have two choices. Either they try to figure out how to borrow all the money to get their student through the last two years of college, or they simply bring the student back home and put him in a cheaper university. In the worst-case scenario, the student just quits. As a matter of fact, that's the number one reason students quit college: the parents run out of money and can't afford to pay. In many cases, this also means they don't have the cash flow to repay a loan, so borrowing is out of the question. Each fall, 2.8 million students enroll in some form of higher education, but fewer than half of the students who start school graduate within six years, according to the

NOT GOOD

SENU
Southwest
Northwoods
University

Office of Financial Aid Scholarships
Southeast Northwoods University, 12345 Gerald Building, Markham, WA 98520
Telephone 360-555-1212 | Fax 360-555-1213 | Email financialaid@senorthwoods.edu

(F)

2013-2014
FINANCIAL AID AWARD

Date:	07-APR-13
Student ID:	
Class Level	Junior
Budget Status:	Non-Resident
Dependency Status:	Dependent

Dear

We are pleased to offer you a **2013-2014** financial aid award to assist you in financing your education at Southeast Northwoods U. You may accept this offer by returning a signed copy of this letter OR by accepting the award on-line using Student Online Services. Parent PLUS loans require a separate application for a credit decision.

Est. Cost of Attendance(COA)

Expected Family Contribution (EFC)		Resources
Parent Contribution	7,051	
Student Contribution	140	

EST. TOTAL COA =	$0	Total EFC =	$7,191	Total Resources	$0
NEED = COA minus EFC minus RESOURCES				Need =	$0

Your Aid Offer:

Accept	Reject	Revise	Financial Aid Programs	Summer	Fall	Winter	Spring	TOTAL
		N/A	Tuition Grant/Need/NonResident	0	1,500	1,500	1,500	4,500
			Federal Ford Direct Loan-Sub	0	1,833	1,833	1,834	5,500
			Federal Ford Direct Loan-unsub	0	667	667	666	2,000
N/A	N/A	N/A	Tuition Grant Scholarship	0	667	667	666	2,000

	TOTAL AID OFFER	$0	$4,667	$4,667	$4,666	$14,000

YOU MUST EITHER RETURN A SIGNED PAPER COPY OR ACCEPT ONLINE
BY 05/05/2013 OR YOUR OFFER WILL BE CANCELED
View/accept your award on-line at: Accept Award Offer by Aid Year

(Accept Awards)

 VIEW CONDITIONS OF AWARD AT: University 1

US Department of Education. At public community colleges, only 20 percent of students graduate within three years.

When I speak on the topic of financial aid in my workshops, I tend to get on a soapbox. I'm really passionate about this because too many families are unaware of this practice, especially at well-known schools. Note: Just because they are well-known doesn't automatically make them good schools. However, in this case, the college that provided this award letter is popular in the United States. It has some good programs. It's also a big-time football school. But it has a bad habit of not giving families a lot of free money. And it gives returning students little time to figure out what to do about it. An incoming freshman will usually receive an award letter around May. Returning students, at some schools, don't get their award letters until June or July, after all the freshmen have received theirs.

For the family who received this award letter, I was able to, despite the short time frame, appeal the award. The school eventually came back with more money in the second award letter. At that point, they had two students in college, which automatically lowered the expected family contribution. But for some strange reason, they initially ignored that fact. The following year, the school gave them a lot more money, but the initial offer was quite poor. **Grade: F**

University 2

At first glance, this award looks like a good offer. The financial-aid officers at the school gave a pretty big scholarship of $14,000. They also gave a grant of $2,000, so the total gift was $16,530. The cost of attendance at this school is about $50,000, and the EFC is about $40,000, so it looks like this family's need of $10,000 is more than met.

But how exactly is it being met? Notice the Parent PLUS Loan—it amounts to nearly $27,000. The offer also features an unsubsidized loan of $6,500. That's what makes this a bad offer. One of the things I don't want to see in award letters is a ton of PLUS loans. Why? Remember, the PLUS loan is the parent loan for undergraduate students. PLUS loans

Not Good

FINANCIAL AID AWARD LETTER

Northern
Bellevue
University

Financial Aid Office • 6500 W Williamson Pkwy • Bellevue WA 98008 • 425-555-9080 • financialaid@unibelle.edu

April 23, 2013

UPID   001574957
Aid Year: 2013-14
Student Type: Undergrad
Award Type: ORIGINAL

We are pleased to offer you the following estimated financial assistance to attend the Northern Bellevue U. This award letter is based on information available at the time of awarding and supersedes all previous award letters. This aid is subject to the terms and conditions listed in the Northern Bellevue U Financial Aid Handbook available at unibelle.edu/2/financial-aid. Aid is based on full-time status unless otherwise indicated in the Financial Aid Messages section on the back of this letter.

Award Details

Gift Aid	SUMMER	FALL	SPRING	TOTAL
J.P. Vollmers Scholarship		$7,000.00	$7,000.00	$14,000.00
Northern Bellevue U Grant		$1,265.00	$1,265.00	$2,530.00
Total Gift Aid:				**$16,530.00**
Self-Help Aid				
Parent PLUS Loan		$13,495.00	$13,495.00	$26,990.00
Stafford Unsubsidized Loan		$3,250.00	$3,250.00	$6,500.00
Total Self-Help Aid:				**$33,490.00**
Total Financial Aid Offered		**$25,010.00**	**$25,010.00**	**$50,020.00**

Calculation of Financial Need
This financial aid offer is based on calculations using an estimated **Cost of Attendance** which generally includes tuition, fees, room & board, books & supplies, transportation, and personal expenses. Included in this calculation is a federally-determined **Expected Family Contribution**. These values are used in the following manner to determine your eligibility for need-based financial aid, **Cost of Attendance - Expected Family Contribution = Need**. The amounts are shown below.

Cost of Attendance: $50,020.00   Expected Family Contribution: $40,401.00   Need: $9,619.00

Once your eligibility for need-based aid is determined, the Office of Financial Aid attempts to fill it with different types of available awards, including gift and self-help aid. Because funding is limited, we may not be able to fill your entire need.

***** Complete the **Self-Help Aid Table** on the back. Sign and return one copy to the Office of Finan. University 2
Page 1 of 2

can't be forgiven. If you take a parent loan, for example, for $50,000 to get your child through college instead of the student taking out $50,000 in loans, you won't get the chance to take advantage of loan-forgiveness programs. If your child were to find a job that has loan forgiveness or is offered employment with loan forgiveness as an enticement, the company would forgive the student of his or her loans, but they're not going to forgive you, the parent, of your loans.

So this financial-aid offer is not good mainly because there's too much of a loan involved. It's a big loan for the parents to take on—bigger than the price of a brand-new car. **Grade: D**

University 3

This offer is also from a well-known school. It's in the Midwest, and it has a pretty good endowment fund. It's not a big sports school but is well known for its technology programs. This family, a single-income household making less than $80,000 a year, had two students in this college at the same time. With two students in college, their Expected Family Contribution came in pretty low, but to make up their need, the family was offered loans in the award letter. The grant scholarship part was fine, but I would have rather seen more work study or more of a scholarship or need-based grant at the top of the award instead of the large PLUS loan. I felt that they could've done better based on what I've seen similar schools do under similar circumstances.

The award was appealed, but the school came back and said, "No, we're not going to do anything extra." This happens sometimes. Most colleges are OK with appeals, but other colleges might look at the appeal as a sob story. They would prefer that you suck it up and figure out how to pay. A family can also decide to go to a different school. However, this family stayed. They felt that having both of their children at the same school was much better than having them go elsewhere and then having to deal with some other circumstances. **Grade: C**

OK

MIDWEST GLOBAL
TECHNOLOGY UNIVERSITY

Student ID

Estimated Expenses: 2009-10	
Tuition	$28,512.00
Fees	$844.00
Room and Board	$9,704.00
Books and Supplies	$1,000.00
Total Estimated Expenses	**$40,060.00**

www.midglo.edu

Financial Aid Services
1900 West Central Dr
Suite 908-B
Hammond, IN 46320

800.555.3423
financial@midglo.edu

FAFSA Code:
0019282093

Grants and Scholarships	Fall	Spring	Total
Wellington Scholarship	$5,000.00	$5,000.00	$10,000.00
Need-Based Grant	$1,900.00	$1,900.00	$3,800.00
University Scholarship	$3,500.00	$3,500.00	$7,000.00
Total Grants and Scholarships			**$20,800.00**
Loans			
Federal Parent Loan	$4,630.00	$4,630.00	$9,260.00
Federal Perkins Loan	$1,000.00	$1,000.00	$2,000.00
Federal Subsidized Stafford Loan	$1,750.00	$1,750.00	$3,500.00
Federal Unsubsidized Stafford Loan	$1,000.00	$1,000.00	$2,000.00
Total Loans			**$16,760.00**
Student Employment			
Federal Work Study	$1,250.00	$1,250.00	$2,500.00
Total Student Employment			**$2,500.00**
Total Financial Aid			**$40,060.00**

[1] Fees include Service Fee, U-PASS (The University Pass provides unlimited access to the City's public transportation), and Activity Fee.
[2] Housing costs will vary depending upon living arrangements.
[3] Books and Supplies - Architecture students might have additional expenses for materials.
[4] Health Insurance, transportation, and personal expenses are not included. A health insurance fee will be added to your bill unless you show proof of coverage through an existing carrier.

Page 2

University 3

University 4

This offer is pretty decent. The school awarded good scholarship money, some subsidized and unsubsidized direct loans, and work study. The total award came out to roughly $22,000 a year. They didn't put any parent loans in the offer. The family's EFC was pretty high, higher than most families can afford, but the school met their need very well.

Good

Atlantis ♆
University

2013-2014 FINANCIAL AID AWARD NOTIFICATION

Ⓑ

March 14, 2013

We are pleased to offer you the following financial aid to help fund your education at Atlantis University in 2013-2014.

Gift aid	Fall	Spring	TOTAL
Trustee Scholarship	$5,750.00	$5,750.00	$11,500.00
Timesetter Scholarship	$1,000.00	$1,000.00	$2,000.00
Atlantis Grant	$750.00	$750.00	$1,500.00
Self-Help aid			
Federal Direct Subsidized Loan	$1,750.00	$1,750.00	$3,500.00
Federal Direct Unsubsidized Loan	$1,000.00	$1,000.00	$2,000.00
Federal Work-Study	$1,000.00	$1,000.00	$2,000.00
Total award	**$11,250.00**	**$11,250.00**	**$22,500.00**

Your award amounts were determined based on $37,024 in tuition and fees, $10,792 for room and board, and additional amounts for books, transportation, and other costs for a total Cost of Attendance of $50,486. Your actual costs will vary based on your personal spending and other factors. PLEASE NOTE: if you were awarded work-study, those funds must be earned and will not be available to pay billed charges; and any loans you choose to borrow will require you to sign a promissory note and must be repaid with interest.

Parents of *dependent* undergraduates who need additional funds may apply for a Federal Direct Parent PLUS Loan for up to the Cost of Attendance minus financial aid received. Careful budgeting may allow borrowing less than the maximum available.

If you were awarded Federal loans, please sign and return one copy of this Financial Aid Award Notification to the Pacific University Financial Aid Office. We **MUST** have a signed award notification on file before we can process your federal loans. Please refer to the **Financial Aid Checklist** for important additional information.

_____   _____   _____
Student Name   Student Signature   Date

If you want to decline or accept a reduced amount of loans or other awards, please request the reduction(s) below. **Please note: be sure to decline or reduce *unsubsidized loans* before subsidized loans.**

Loan	Reduce Total Amount To
Federal Direct Unsubsidized Loan	$_____
Federal Direct Subsidized Loan	$_____
Other _____	$_____

University 4

Now, why was this school able to present a better offer? Simply put, I think they really wanted the student. If a college really wants your child as a student, they're going to meet your need, and sometimes they will give you more than you need. They'll go above the norm just to get that student at that school. Schools sometimes compete to see which one wants the student more in terms of giving out the money; plus, the school needs to fill seats. This is where leveraging is happening in favor of a family. In this case, they gave this student a lot of money, but then other students who might have the same EFC don't get so much because the school needs to balance out its budget with the plethora of different students. It's like an airplane seat—the students are sitting in the same row, but none of them paid the same price to be there. **Grade: B**

University 5

This school's award letter makes a fine offer and gets an A+ for it. The total cost of the education was $54,896, and they gave the family $41,900, but with no PLUS loans. Also—and this is pretty big—they offered a four-year scholarship based on merit, not need. That's $23,000 guaranteed every single year. The loan amounts aren't that high, and they are all student loans, not parent loans. This is great because it means that in certain employment situations, the student's loans can qualify for forgiveness. There's also a work study amount here that's not included in the actual award, so that's in addition to everything else. That brings the family's cost down even more.

An $11,400 grant they offered is a yearly grant based on need. This was a single-parent home, so the family's income wasn't that high. As long as the income remains at a certain level because of the way things are going in the economy or in their line of work, then the student will be fine. But if the parent gets a pay raise, ends up making a lot more money, or gets married, then the story will change. Those factors must be taken into consideration and planned for. Again, this is the very first year of the student going away to college. What makes this really special is that the college is a top-notch institution and a private university. So paying $13,000 a year for a school of this caliber is a super good deal! **Grade: A+**

GREAT !   (A+)

L. JEFFERSON
UNIVERSITY

2014–15 FINANCIAL AID AWARD

03/17/14
Student ID:

AWARD PROGRAMS	FALL	SPRING	TOTAL	
L. Jefferson University Scholarship	11,500.00	11,500.00	23,000.00	
Federal Direct Subsidized Loan	1,750.00	1,750.00	3,500.00	
L. Jefferson University Grant	5,700.00	5,700.00	11,400.00	
Federal Perkins Loan	1,000.00	1,000.00	2,000.00	
Federal Direct Unsubsidized Loan	1,000.00	1,000.00	2,000.00	
Total aid available	**20,950.00**	**20,950.00**	**$41,900.00**	

The total estimated cost of attendance for 2014-15, which includes tuition, fees, room and board, is $54,896.00.

If you accept your entire financial aid offer and live on campus, the remainder of total costs for which you are responsible is approximately $12,996.00.

In addition, please budget approximately $980 for books and supplies during the academic year.

You are also eligible for Federal Work Study. For additional information about finding a position, please visit our website at http://l-jefferson.edu/area1/careers. You are eligible to earn up to the following amount:

Federal Work-Study Program	1,250.00	1,250.00	2,500.00

If you have any questions, please contact us at 909-909-9009, or toll-free at 800-555-9009. Ou **University 5** are Monday through Friday, 8:00 am to 5:00 pm.

Once You Have the Letter, What Next?

When the award letter arrives, you'll have, at best, only about a month and at worse, about two or three weeks to decide whether or not to accept or to decline the offer. This can make it extremely difficult because that is a short period of time in which to make such a big decision. The way to combat this situation is to take action steps based on the award letters you receive. For example, it is paramount to choose several schools that are industry leaders for a particular major. Having a backup plan will provide you with several good options so you won't be forced into a corner. As you make your decision, here's something to watch out for: *Some schools are going to misaward you on purpose.* They might give you more money than you qualify for. If the school does this, you simply take the money because it means that they really want your student.

On the other hand, some schools are going to underaward you, which means they're going to give you way less money than you qualify for. That was the case with University 1 in our examples. They offered the student's family an amount much lower than what they were eligible for. The family's EFC was $7,000, and their need was $35,000, but the school offered only $14,000 in aid.

Again, some schools will try to compete with other schools for your student. Once you complete your FAFSA, the system will generate a student-aid report. That report will get sent to all of the colleges your child applied to because when you fill out your FAFSA, you have to list those schools.

Let's say we're looking at College 1, College 2, College 3, and College 4. If one school thinks it has a better shot at getting your student versus those other schools and really wants that student, it is likely that the school will offer more aid.What some parents do—and I don't condone this—is say, "College 1 offered me $10,000 more, but my student really wants to go to your school (College 3), so could you please match what College 1 gave us?" There's an underlying message behind that because College 3 can come back and say, "We don't think your student is a good fit for our school. Maybe that's why College 1 offered more. It appears that College 1 really wants your child and feels that he is a really good fit for the university. We highly suggest that you take College 1's offer because we're not going to give you more. If we thought your child would be a good fit here, you would've received money in the acceptance letter we provided you."

The bottom line is this: if a school really wants a particular student, the decision makers won't make the family wait to see an award letter. They will mention money right off the bat in the acceptance letter. It might say something like, "Congratulations! Because of your hard work and diligence, we're going to award you $15,000 per year over the next four years." That's $60,000, and it's in the acceptance letter. It's actually in addition to whatever you would receive in your financial-need award letter. But if you don't get money in the acceptance letter and you're waiting for your award letter, then that's kind of a bad sign to get accepted to a school with no money. The caveat to this is if the school is a CSS PROFILE school. These schools tend to meet 100 percent of a family's need. That's determined based on your financial information, which they obtain though the financial-aid process.

When you do get your award letter, you might say, " Harold, we feel that our award letter is really unfair. We're going to appeal it." If that's your take on the situation, you must know two things:

1. How to talk to the people in the financial-aid offices
2. That an appeal is easier said than done

You must understand that if you're going to appeal your award letter, it's like appealing a decision by the court. First of all, you have to have grounds for an appeal. Just saying, "Your school is too expensive, so I need more money," is not going to cut it. There has to be some sort of circumstance that you didn't outline in your FAFSA form because they do have a special-circumstances section that allows you to explain your situation. A lot of people simply fill out the forms and send them to the school, but they don't know how to explain their financial situation because they don't know exactly what it is the school is looking for to reverse the package it offered. Most people don't know how to say what needs to be said, and they don't know how to say it or how to put it on the forms. Indicating that you have information that was not communicated earlier is very, very important.

When I write an appeal letter, it is based on certain things such as proving that you were under-awarded based on your EFC. You have to know what to ask for in the appeal letter, and you have to be very specific regarding your situation. In many cases, when I've written the appeal letter, the college comes back with an extra $3,000 or $4,000, on average. That's not bad, considering that my fee for services breaks down to an amount lower than your family's monthly cable or cell phone bill, which I've seen at about $250 for each! If I can save you $3,000 to $4,000 every year for four years, I'd say that's a pretty good deal.

But there is a danger to initiating an appeal. You could open up yourself for further investigation. In other words, the school might say, "We really want to see what's going on. Send us your last five years' tax returns." You might have done something five years back to position yourself so that you're in this situation, and it could've been avoided. Colleges have business offices now that will look over tax returns and paper trails. They can put two and two together and see that something just doesn't add up in your story. If you try to get money out of the school fraudulently, they can turn you in, and you will face a whole lot of other circumstances for failing to be forthcoming with all the information. When I do appeals, I always ask the parents, "Is there anything in your past that I should know about? Have you done anything that really needs to be disclosed?" You've got to be up-front with me because if you're not and we get caught, I'm going to be in just as big a trouble as you are.

The End Game

But remember, such extra measures won't be necessary if you plan well from the beginning. This is kind of like watching a football game with your favorite team playing. Your team has been stinking up the game for four quarters. They've not been playing up to their ability, nor are they doing everything they have to do. Then they're down to the last minute, and they go to the hurry-up offense. They have to score—and fast! The quarterback throws a pass, and there's pass interference, but the referee doesn't call it. The game is lost based on something happening at the end. That could have been avoided if they had played better in the first three quarters.

At this stage of the game, you really don't want to leave it up to a financial-aid officer to tell you, "Hey, your chances of getting your student through college are pretty slim, and we flat-out can't help you." The truth is, there are a lot of things that could've and should've been done that weren't. I do my best to remain sympathetic to a family's situation because I don't know everything that they've gone through or what happened them that led to their current set of circumstances. The reality is that when you get to this point, you're at the mercy of the financial-aid officer if you haven't planned accordingly. Your child's future is at the mercy of one person who could be very impartial to you. She may not be sympathetic because this is a business, and she feels that you've had seventeen years to sit down and figure out, "If my student is going to go to college, what do we do?"

I hear this from a lot of people: "The reason why we didn't do anything is because we weren't sure what our child was going to do."

Then I'll ask the question, "Whose responsibility is it, anyway? Is it your child's responsibility to decide his future, or is it something you do for him along the way, and you give him options?" It's really not about "if" your child decides to go to college; it's a question of where he's going to go. Again, this is a conversation you strike up with your child from a young age. Then you build in these expectations along the way. A lot of parents fail to plan just because they didn't build in these expectations for their children. Proper planning for college can make all the difference in the world.

CHAPTER 6

What Can Reduce Your Financial-Aid Award?

Planning to pay for a college education requires a certain amount of diligence. On some level, we all know that. Reading this book is a form of due diligence on your part—you're seeking to learn as much as possible that will help you be smart about this all-important journey.

We've covered the importance of getting the application process right the first time and why you must get the forms submitted as soon as possible. I know you'll want to act on the information you find in this book because it is helpful. However, now I want to discuss other advice or strategies you may be following that could actually hinder this process and hurt your chances for financial aid. It's important to discuss because many families try to follow the advice they've received in the name of being diligent—they fund certain college savings programs and try to save money in a certain way. People in certain income brackets are being told that such programs are their saving grace to pay for college. I get the question all the time, "Harold, what am I doing that's killing my chances to get financial aid?" Here are some of the issues to consider.

Making What Seems Like Too Much at the Wrong Time

This one is somewhat of a catch-22. Currently the

average age of parents I work with who are sending their first child off to college is fifty-two to fifty-five years of age. In this age bracket, these parents have become successful in their careers. They may be in upper-level management and may be making between $125,000 and $250,000 annually. It's possible, depending on the family's situation, that they have too much income. Let me clarify this. Making $125,000 to $250,000 doesn't necessary put you out of range for some sort of financial aid.

I find that many families at this stage may have a high income, but they don't have assets, and this proves to be somewhat problematic. You may be wondering, *Why does a person with that much income not have assets?*

They didn't start out with that much income. They probably got married between the ages of twenty-five and thirty. Their first child was born when they were, say, thirty-two or thirty-three. That's why they're fifty-two and sending their first seventeen-year-old off to college. I guess you could say life happened, right? They bought a house, and then they had other children, and then they had to buy a bigger home. Along the way, they've been putting funds into their IRAs and their 401(k)s. They've been thinking about retirement, but they have not saved much money for college. Again, 66 percent of their net worth is sitting in IRAs and 401(k)s. Or they could've even invested in a rental property, and cash could be tied up in that.

You may be asking yourself, "Should I take a pay cut or quit my job for financial aid?" Depending on your situation, that could be an option. I've seen cases in which a family's financial situation actually improved by opting for an earlier retirement due to being offered buyouts and things of that sort.

But to outright quit your job for aid, I would say definitely not.

Too Many Assets?

On the flip side is a trickier situation—too many assets. I say it's tricky because it's not what you might think. I say "too many assets," and you may start thinking about rental properties or second homes. But really this is more about smaller items you might not even consider to be assets. In fact, I call this situation "too much, but not enough." It means you have an asset that is considered too large to help you qualify for financial aid, but the amount of the asset is not enough to cover the entire cost of college. In that situation, I'll see a family come in who is making $110,000 between both parents. On the basis of their income alone, they would qualify for some financial aid, but what tends to hurt them is the Christmas account Grandma has given them or a CD that an uncle or aunt has set aside for the child. The amount of such accounts is not enough to cover the entire cost of college, but, in many cases, the mere existence of this money is hurting the family's chances for financial aid. They would be much better off not having it.

I tend to ask my clients, "Are your grandparents or your parents going to help pay for college?" Many of them will say, "No, they don't have any money." But I make it clear to them they must be careful about accepting money—this is extremely serious. They say, "No, they don't have any money," but then the grandparents will begin to slip cash to them here and there. In some cases, depending on how they give that money to the family, it could be counted as income. Gift tax implications and other problems could come into play.

Let's say we have a situation in which we've gotten you

and your family into the best position possible so that you're getting $10,000 to $15,000, maybe even $20,000 in financial aid. All of a sudden, an audit or a 1099 is generated, and then the school sees that extra cash coming in from a grandparent. That new income could potentially cause you to lose the financial aid you've been getting.

However, that could have been a one-time thing when the grandparents said, "You know what? We have thirty thousand dollars. We're going to give it to you this year." If we're alerted to this, we can decide whether or not it's a good year for the family to receive such funds. We will ask if additional funds will be coming in from anywhere else. If so, it might be better to receive the $30,000 the following year or not to take the money at all. But we need to know this so we can account for it. No matter how good the intentions are, a large monetary gift could be a devastating thing when we start the financial-aid process.

What About 529 Plans?

When clients ask me about saving for college with 529 plans, I tell them that I'm not for 529 plans. I'm not against them. They're an excellent tool for some people; they're just not for everyone.

The 529 plan was created by the states back in the late '80s to help families offset the high cost of college. It provided parents with an incentive to save money. The benefits of the 529 plan are, in some cases, pretty amazing, depending on when you're in the market. If you're in a bull market and you're investing in a 529 plan, it's pretty awesome because the cash can just sit in there and grow tax-free. When you take it out and use it for college, all of the gain is tax-free.

That's a great tax benefit for people who are in high income brackets who otherwise would not be eligible for financial aid.

I'll give you an example. Let's say a family is making $250,000 to $300,000 a year. Depending on the school, that family may not qualify for need-based financial aid, so they can set aside funds in a 529 plan. I've seen as much as $300,000 in a 529 plan. And, depending on where that student wants to go to college, it could pretty much take care of the whole thing.

However, on the flip side, the average 529 plan in the United States contains only about $20,000 to $25,000. Many families who come in to see us have 529 plan accounts with this amount. For many people, that won't cover even the first year of college. So how does the account affect their chances for financial aid? It depends on how the asset is held. If the 529 plan is held in the parents' name, it's counted at a different percentage than if the 529 plan is held in the student's name.

When colleges look at the account, they'll see whether it's a parental asset or an asset that belongs to the student. In some cases, they could look at that 529 plan and say, "OK, spend down that 529 plan in the first year and then come back the second year, and we'll see how much aid to give you." That might not sound fair, and I'm not saying all colleges do this. However, when colleges go through the financial-aid process, they do have rules. They have guidelines and budgets to meet as well. But remember what usually happens in that second year. We talked earlier about how colleges give the best financial-aid package in the first year. If you don't get it right the first time and you have money sitting around that could hurt you, then your chances of getting additional aid the next year go down tremendously. It's better to understand how that 529 plan is going to help or hurt you, depending on your situation.

The 529 Caveats

I have some caveats about 529 plans, and one of them is this: 5 percent of the people who have them should have them only because of what I said earlier. They are the high-income people, the top 1 or 5 percent of income earners, who would benefit the most from this program. For the average person making between $50,000 and $100,000 a year, the 529 plan may do more harm than good because he or she simply can't put away what a high income earner could put into the 529 plan to make it worthwhile. In that person's situation, it may be better not to have it.

But don't read this and think, *Oh, I make seventy-five thousand a year, so I'm not going to start a 529 plan.* Why? Because I can't say with 100 percent accuracy that that is a good strategy for you until I look at your family's particular financial situation. I would never just automatically say, "You should have one" or "You should not have one." Many factors affect the decision. I'm also saying don't just automatically consider a 529 plan as your number one savings bucket for college.

The other caveat to the 529 plan is this: What if the market takes a down turn at the time you need the funds the most? What's the backup plan? Many people don't have one, so they end up raiding the asset they have the easiest access to.

I've also found many people having a tough time when it comes to taking funds from their 529s to pay for college. I'll provide an example. A family decided to hire my firm to work with them. In creating their plan to pay for college they felt it was best to use the 529 plan in the student's first year to get it over with. When they went to their financial advisor to request the funds, he told them, "You know, right now wouldn't be a good time to take the funds out because the market isn't performing so well. You should leave the funds in the 529 plan and let them recover." When asked what they should do, to their amazement, the advisor told them to borrow on their home. At that point, they felt they should've just paid the house down from the beginning versus losing the money in the stock market. At least the equity in their home would've been there, guaranteed.

Because this happens to families quite a bit, let me say this: be careful if you go to a planner for help with paying for college and they say right off the bat you should have a 529 plan. In this business, a 529 plan is kind of like the doctor hitting your knee to check your reflexes. A planner will reel off these plans, the 529s, UGMAs, UTMAs, without considering whether or not they are truly right for you because those are the resources they know about to solve the college funding problem. UGMA stands for Uniform Gifts to Minors Act. UTMA stands for Uniform Transfers to Minors Act. They are all part of the kiddie tax rules that basically govern how a parent can shift income. In other words, people have assets that generate income. That income puts them in a higher tax bracket. The parents can shift certain assets like stocks, bonds, and mutual funds to their children because the children are in a lower tax bracket, and they'll pay taxes at a much lower rate than the parents have to.

This was all part of the $1.35 trillion **Economic Growth and Tax Relief Reconciliation Act of 2001**. It was Congress's way of trying to help families tackle the rising cost of college. There are a number of pieces connected to this act that you should know about, especially in terms of the taxes that directly affect your education cost.

Hope Scholarship Credit/American Opportunity Credit

When you take this credit on your tax return, a portion of your college cost will be credited back to you. The value could be anywhere between $1,500 to $2,500, depending on your tax situation. Generally, you can claim the Opportunity Credit if all the following requirements are met:

- You pay qualified educational expenses for higher education.
- You pay the educational expenses for an eligible student.
- The eligible student is yourself, your spouse, or a dependent for whom you can claim the exemption on your tax return. (See irs.gov publications, p. 970 in the IRS tax code).

There are different phase-outs related to this eligibility. For example, people who are making a high income can't claim the credit. Your tax advisor will need a good grasp of the whole situation.

Lifetime Learning Credit

For each tax year, you may be able to claim this credit of up to $2,000 for qualified education expenses paid for all eligible students. There is no limit on the number of years the lifetime learning credit can be claimed for each student.

Because you can't claim this credit in addition to the Opportunity Credit or a Student Loan Interest Rate Deduction, you'll want to know which deduction will work out best for your situation.

The Student Loan Interest Rate Deduction

Generally, personal interest you pay on auto loans or credit cards is not deductible on your tax return. However, if your modified adjusted gross income (MAGI) is less than $75,000 ($155,000 if filing a joint return) you can take a special deduction for paying interest on a student loan used for higher education. This deduction can reduce the amount of your income subject to tax by up to $2,500.

Coverdell ESAs

These were formerly called "educational IRAs." If your MAGI is less than $110,000 ($220,000 if filing a joint return), you can establish a Coverdell ESA to finance the qualified education expenses of a designated beneficiary.

Penalty-Free IRA Withdrawals

Many of my clients have heard about penalty-free IRA withdrawals, so they come to me and ask, "Should I take money out of my IRA or my 401(k) to pay for college? I heard someone say I could do that, and there are no penalties whatsoever on those funds coming out." On one level, they are absolutely correct. If you take the cash out of your IRA or 401(k), it is penalty-free. However, there is another hidden penalty you won't see, and that is the penalty to your financial aid.

How does that happen? Let's say you have $100,000 in your IRA or your 401(k) and you take $10,000 out penalty-free. You have to claim that $10,000 as income. If we go back and look at the FAFSA in terms of how they determine your eligibility for financial aid, it's cost of attendance minus EFC equals your need. Your expected family contribution is based on income, age, the number of people in school, and a host of other factors, income being one of the biggest things. A lot of times, people freak out. They don't know what to do. They haven't planned well for college, and they have all this money in their IRA. They'll say, "You know what? If I have to cash in my retirement account to get Jimmy through school, I'll do that." What they end up doing is taking out cash for the first or second year, and then they're pretty much done taking cash out because they realize that was a mistake. Here's why.

Those funds from the IRA are counted as income against you, which then *increases* your expected family contribution. So in many cases, you're better off not doing that, even though it's penalty-free. Remember, colleges give out the best aid package in the very first year. If you have a 529 plan that's in the student's name and now you're taking out cash from your IRA to cover the cost of college, you can pretty much see how you're going to shoot yourself in the foot and not get any financial aid for the rest of the time your children are in college, depending on the school they attend.

Employee Education Assistance Plan

If you receive educational assistance benefits from your employer under an educational assistance program, you can exclude up to $5,250 of those benefits each year. This means your employer should not include those benefits with your wages, tips, and other compensation shown in box 1 of your Form W-2. This also means that you do not have to include the benefits on your income tax return.

With this plan, your employer could also get a tax deduction for helping you send your child to college. However, that plan has to be in place, and it has to be a nondiscriminatory plan. In other words, the company can't discriminate against the highly compensated employees of the corporation versus the lower compensated employees. Everyone has to have the right to participate in the plan. It has to be equal across the board.

Qualified State Prepaid Tuition Tax Advantages

With these qualified state prepaid tuition programs, you can place cash into a program that will prepay the tuition for a school in that state. The main attraction of this program is that it keeps the tuition the same during each year of your child's college education. You wouldn't have to pay a higher tuition because it's all paid up front. The costs stay the same for you for all four years, and you don't have to worry about the rising cost of inflation on the cost of education.

However, some risks are associated with frontloading this type of program. For example, what if your child doesn't go to school in that state? There's no guarantee he or she will get into a college in that particular state. You also have to consider the lost opportunity cost of having the money working for you now versus being tied up in the plan.

Credit or Deduction?

As I said earlier, you usually have to choose among tax benefits. You can't take a credit as well as a deduction. You have to choose which one will be more beneficial to your financial picture. But how do you figure that out? When we look at the tax credits versus the tax deductions, the tax deductions will reduce your taxable income. For example, a thousand dollar tax deduction in a 28 percent tax bracket saves you only $280 in taxes. The tax credit, on the other hand, reduces income tax. A $1,000 tax credit in any tax bracket saves you $1,000 on taxes. So, when people ask, "Should I choose one or the other?" I'll say, "Talk to your CPA," but I'd probably take the tax credit over the tax deduction any day. Again, you have to know your situation.

Asking the Right Questions

Getting the maximum money for college under the confusing and complicated rules of the Tax Relief Reconciliation Act is no easy task. You will have to ask yourself a lot of questions before you start planning for college. You need to know these things far in advance. Here are a few questions you'll want to consider.

1. Will taking advantage of one of the new tax revisions actually cost me money by reducing the amount of aid I would otherwise qualify for?

If you were to put money into an UTMA account, an UGMA account, or a 529 plan, where are you going to be when your student actually goes away to college? Are you going to be in a higher income bracket or a lower income tax bracket? Will you have more assets? Will you have fewer assets? What is the cost of college going to be? Without knowing all this, it's really hard to plan.

2. Should I refinance my home to pay for college?

When I teach this material in live workshops, I often ask,

"How many of you would refinance your home to pay for college?" Everyone in the room looks at me like I just said a bad word. One or two of them may say, "You know what? I'll do whatever it takes to send my child to college, even if I have to sell my house and live in a tent." Other people will say, "Harold, I'm not going to refinance my home to pay for college because this is my child's problem, and she's going to have to figure out how to pay for it on her own. I'm not doing that."

There is no right or wrong answer to this question because that's a personal opinion. It's all up to the family values, what's important to you. Is your child's education so important to you that you would sell your home and live in a tent? It's a firestorm or a fire starter, depending on how and to whom you ask the question.

Here are a few more questions: Do you qualify for or should you start a Coverdell ESA? What are the restrictions on IRAs for college expenses? Qualified state tuition programs are a viable option, but is it right for your situation? These are questions you will have to answer before getting involved in the process.

If you can't answer such questions, you shouldn't get started. Why? Because if you start your plan without having these questions answered, are you going to be able to jump ship and do something different when you find out something contrary to what you thought earlier? If so, what are the cost ramifications? For example, if you start an UTMA account for your child because you know that's going to help get the money out of your name, it's a tax situation now. You're trying to avoid taxes by putting money in your child's name. Your child then goes to college and you say, "Hey, I just learned that the UTMA account is not a good thing. I should just take that

money and put it back in my name because the percentage is
counted lower on my assets." But you can't do that. It's illegal
because it's the child's asset. You can't just take your child's
assets and put them back in your name. Many parents think
they can do this because someone told them, "Just take the
cash out and pay your bills off with that." Be careful. A lot of
wrong ideas are floating around out there with regard to planning for college. You don't want to become a casualty of the
Economic Growth and Tax Relief Reconciliation Act.

Proper Financial Planning: Who Can Help?

I've stressed the importance of starting your financial
and tax planning early, long before most parents realize
they have to start thinking about college. It may seem like a
daunting task, but it's a lot easier if you have the right people
helping you. But who is the "right person"? I'll discuss that
here because it can be confusing. You may think you have
the right person because he or she is a whiz at accounting
and tax preparation. But that person may not be knowledge-
able about the ins and outs of college funding. She may
give you advice that is perfectly valid without realizing the
strategy could affect the amount of financial aid you qualify for. *You want to be sure the professional you choose is
completely aware of the required integration and coordina-
tion necessary between your tax situation and your college
funding situation.*

Here's what can happen if you don't have the right professional. One of the things we find is that when people come
in and say they've been working with their CPA, I'll ask, "OK,
what did your CPA say to do?" It turns out the CPA is doing a
great job helping them reduce their taxes. She has the client

in UTMAs and UGMAs and had the family start a 529 plan. These strategies will help reduce taxes. But in many cases, these people are putting themselves in situations in which they're reducing their taxes now, but it's going to kill their chances for financial aid later. What happens in those situations? Many of these families end up having to borrow on their homes, borrow from their IRAs, and borrow from their 401(k)s. Why? Because they put the money in places that are not right for the college funding situation.

What about School Counselors?

I know you may be reading this and asking yourself, *Can't the colleges or the high school guidance counselors or college career counselors help me with this? Why wouldn't they be able to? Why wouldn't it be in their best interest to give me the best possible counseling to get the maximum funding for college?* Remember, theory is different from reality. Let me explain.

They should be able to help, but unfortunately, most of them don't or can't fully help you get the maximum amount of funding. Asking colleges to help you with financial aid or to help you get more money from their particular school is like asking an IRS agent, "Can you help me with tax planning strategies?" It's not going to happen. The school has a limited amount of funds to give out to large number of people, and they're not going to say, "Here are ten different ways you can pay less out of your pocket and get more funds out of our pocket."

Schools are businesses. They have multibillion-dollar budgets they have to meet all across the board, for everything from football programs and coaches to building maintenance and employee health care. They are responsible for a lot of things. They are not going to tell you, "Here's more money just for you." They'll probably give you some feedback on what to do to apply for aid, but remember, that's putting them in the driver's seat as opposed to yourself. You'll basically be agreeing to get a lot less aid than you could.

The other option is the high school career counselors or the guidance counselors. A lot of people think, *My high school guidance counselor and career counselor said they could help me with this. We have a financial-aid night at our school, so I should be able to get the right advice between the two of them.* But guidance counselors don't have the time to hold your hand through the process. Even if they did, which unfortunately most don't, they're not experts on all of the complicated rules. They're not trained to teach you strategies. They're not trained in every aspect of financial aid and to guide you through the entire process.

I know this for a fact because I happen to have a college counselor as a client. He even went to the financial-aid office at his own child's school and said, "Hey, I need you to help me figure out how to get our children through school. You're the financial-aid people." The financial-aid officer said, "Well, you're kind of on your own. You're going to have to figure out what to do." Now, this is a college counselor asking his financial-aid office what to do because they should know all the ins and the outs and they should be able to help him, right? They were of no help to him at all.

So he found our services and became a client. I admit, I was a little bit leery of taking him on. I thought, *Why do I have a college counselor sitting in front of me? They're the experts in the whole process. Why is he coming to me to help him figure out how to get his two children through college?*

When I asked him these questions directly, his response was quite direct—and surprising. He said, "Harold, I realized that many educational institutions have been selling families short but won't admit it." It was a sad day for him when he came to that realization. With our help, his children are getting through college. One has graduated, and the other will graduate next year.

He was so excited about it. His family's plan is on track. He has bought several new vehicles because now they can afford to and because they needed to. You see, for many years, he and his wife had to put many things on hold for the sake of their children. He's extremely excited about finding us and has referred several families to us. One of the parents happened to be a financial-aid officer at a college. Again, why would a financial-aid officer need help figuring out the financial-aid process if they're experts in the whole process?

I asked her that question.

Her response? "Harold, I understand that that's my job, but we don't know everything."

I said, "You know what? You're the first financial-aid officer who has ever admitted that to me."

How Can You Know What They Know?

If your high school or college counselor says, "We can help you, and here's what you need," you have to find out if that's truly the case. You can do that by asking a series of questions. You may feel uncomfortable grilling the person who is offering to help you, but these questions are important, and you have to ask them.

1. Can you show me how to lower my EFC and maximize my eligibility for aid?

Remember, the formula colleges use is what it is, and no one can change it. You can, however, position yourself to take advantage of what you're truly eligible for. The question is, is that person qualified to help you do that? A better question is, does that person know how?

2. Can you help me pick schools that will (a) give me the best aid package, (b) meet most of my need, (c) give me more free money, and (d) give me fewer loans?

Now, you need to understand what you're asking them to do. You're asking them a financial planning question. Going off to college is an investment, and you're asking an educator about an investment you're going to make in your child's future. In other words, you're going to be footing the bill. Therefore, I feel that that that's not the right question to be asking them. Your question to them in this case should be about one thing and one thing only: admissions, admissions, admissions. A majority of them are pretty good at telling you whether you can or you cannot go to a certain school based on your child's grades.

3. Can you help me fill out the FAFSA and the CSS PRO-FILE forms, line by line?

You could ask and some might say, "Yes, I can help you fill out that form." Well, that's kind of like going to your next door neighbor and saying, "Hey, Jack, you guys do your own taxes. Do you mind sitting down and filling out my tax forms for me?" I don't know if that's something you really want to do. The FAFSA form and the CSS PROFILE form ask for a lot of personal information, and I don't know if you want that college counselor or that financial-aid officer at the school knowing that much about you. That's private information.

4. Will you help me negotiate if I get a bad package or less than I expect from my school?

In this instance, you have to understand something about negotiating. Negotiating with a college is almost like appealing a verdict in a trial. You have to have grounds for an appeal. You can't appeal just because you feel like appealing. The award letter is the same way. You can't call the college and say, "Hey, you gave me a bad aid package or less than I expected. I want more." They're going to tell you, "There's a process we're going to have to send you through, and it's called the appeals process." You're going to have to write letters and so on and so forth. Is a counselor going to have time to help you negotiate at each school? And what if the grounds for your appeal involve a very personal situation? You're dealing with a person at a school who knows hundreds of people. Do you want that person knowing that much about your personal situation, especially if you're not really sure he or she can even help?

5. Can you show me how to pay for college on a tax-favored basis if I don't qualify for financial aid?

I guarantee you, most of them are going to say, "No, that's not my job." If someone does say, "Yeah, we can help you," most likely it's because that person is trying to validate his or her position. Sometimes counselors step over their boundaries and do things they shouldn't do. Let's say, for example, that you work with a counselor and things don't turn out the way you want. You cannot go back the next year and say, "Hey, the advice you gave me was wrong. It didn't work. As a matter of fact, it cost me twenty thousand dollars more than if I had done something different. Can we come back and sue you for that amount?" You have no recourse, and you must understand that prior to letting them help you in this process.

The Right Help: Your Options

You have several options as a parent to find the best guidance to help you through the college planning process. However, I will start off by warning what is not an option: the do-it-yourself method. Trying to figure out how to get a child through four years of college in the most tax-efficient, advantageous way possible is not something you should attempt on your own. If you want to try, the only way you'd have a chance at being successful is if you know these three things in advance:

1. The federal education code
2. The US tax code and how it applies to college
3. The financial planning strategies related to the college planning process

It would take you forty hours or more to learn these different areas and another forty to make them work without getting yourself in trouble. That's eighty hours of work. I don't know any family who has enough time to figure all of this out. Some people say, "You know what? I'm going to take the bull by the horns. I'm going to go to every seminar, every workshop. I'm going to read every book I can."

It is possible. You can do it yourself. You can study and do all the necessary research. Like anything else, if you want to become an expert, if you're willing to devote several hours a week to it over a number of years, you can probably figure this out on your own. I can tell you personally what it takes. I read many publications just to keep up with the process each year, including the major overhauls and the forms. I subscribe to several newsletters. I also attend several meetings each year, and then we read the updated government publications. If you're willing to do this and study the formulas, you may be able to figure it all out on your own, but is it worth your time to do this?

People who get involved in lawsuits don't necessarily try to become legal experts. People have medical issues, but they don't try to become doctors to solve their problems. They usually feel it's worth their time and money to pay a professional who devoted a portion of his or her life learning that area of expertise. It's just easier to let them do what they do and solve the problem for you. The thinking is really no different when it comes to financial planning for college. People pay a number of consultants or experts in most other areas of their life, but suddenly they think they can become an expert at college funding. It doesn't make any sense because you're risking such enormous odds. It seems silly to gamble. Would you be willing to risk $40,000 to $100,000 in funds that your child could have received for his or her education by doing something you have absolutely no experience or expertise in? It amazes me that a lot of parents do just that. They fill out forms, cross their fingers, and hope for the best.

The CPA

Another option is to let your accountant do the college aid

process for you. A lot of people think, *Why not have my CPA do it for me? He is a financial expert who does my taxes, and he probably would do it for me as a favor. This is a good idea.* It seems to be good thinking. But the tax formula is completely different from the financial-aid formula. In fact, doing what you would do for a tax corporation and filling out a tax return is 100 percent different than financial-aid formulas. There are different rules. There are different methods. There are different details you have to look out for. Also, accountants have to apply accounting principles that make sense like. For example, they would recommend strategies like putting your money in your child's name for tax benefits, which we talked about earlier—UGMAs, UTMAs, and 529 plans.

It's going to absolutely kill your chances for financial aid. Unfortunately, most CPAs are not trained in financial-aid preparation or planning. Most accountants are experts at tax prep and tax planning, but they're not financial-aid experts.

The College Funding Consultant

The next and, in my opinion, the best option is to use the services of a college funding consultant or a college financial planner. There is a very small number of people who specialize in college funding consulting. Here in my area, there are only three or four at the most who really understand this process and how it all works. HG Capital is the college financial planning consulting firm who has served our area for the longest period of time.

Our professional association ranks us in the top ten out of three hundred or so college financial planning firms across the country. Our specialty is a little known but very important field. Granted, there are some false prophets out there. The challenge is to find a legitimate specialist who understands all of the rules, regulations, and methodologies.

Don't ask someone to do a scholarship search for you. You want someone who actually understands the way the formulas work, how to negotiate, how to fill out the forms, and how to navigate all of the intricacies of financial aid. Having such a planner is time and money well invested because it will reap you many thousands of dollars in return. This is money you would have never seen or received if you had tried to navigate the financial-aid process on your own.

When you sit down with a college funding planner, the first thing you have to ask is this: "What exactly are you going to do for us?" Any funding planner should know and do the following at the very minimum. He or she should:

1. Be well versed in income and asset planning.
2. Know all of the legal and ethical strategies that are available to you for your specific situation.
3. Know how to work within the realms of the formula to set up your financial picture in a way that maximizes your eligibility for financial aid while also accounting for other financial objectives such as lifestyle and retirement. When you do actually fill out the form, your financial picture should be set up in such a way as to get the best possible package with the lowest out-of-pocket cost.
4. Have an excellent knowledge of the colleges. Your planner should at least have a database of schools and some knowledge about what each school statistically or historically can give in need-based aid, gift aid, and self-help aid. He or she should be able to help you

pick up front the schools that give you the best shot at getting money. This is a critical part in the whole process due to the fact that a lot of schools are constantly changing and evaluating what they give in financial aid each year, depending on their experience. For example, they can give only a limited number of funds to families who have full need, families who have partial need, and families who don't get anything. Schools need to accept a given number out of each one of these categories.

So, based on the applications and the financial experience the school has from a business standpoint and how well its endowments are doing, a school could be more generous from one year to the next. I've seen schools that had a poor history of giving out financial aid. All of a sudden, the school started doing better. They remodeled the campus and hired better professors. Automatically, it became a more desirable place to send children to college. Over time, they became more generous, and now it's one of the most generous schools in the country. Whoever you work with, they should have an understanding of where a school is with this process.

5. Understand how to fill out the forms properly. A lot of people think it's just filling out a form. It's not just filling it out; it's how you fill it out so that it doesn't get bumped back to you. You have to have someone who knows how to fill out the forms properly and will do the major financial-aid forms, including the CSS PROFILE and the FAFSA form. Remember, the information on all of the forms has to be consistent. If the forms aren't

filled out consistently, red flags will pop up, prompting the school to ask for asset verification. If the person who completed the forms for you doesn't really understand what they did that caused these red flags, that can cost you a lot of time and a lot of money, and your child may not even be able to attend that school.

6. Know how to negotiate. This means that they know how to (a) talk to the school in the school's own language and (b) use negotiation letters to increase the package if you are underawarded or misawarded.

The next question you have to ask is very important: "Do you guarantee your results?" My opinion is that any company that is worth anything will be willing to guarantee the results of the plan it created and implemented. This guarantee is exactly as it sounds: if the plan fails to work, you should be entitled to a refund. You should get your money back. I must caution, if you destroy your own plan, there really isn't anyone to blame, and quite frankly, I've seen this happen with families on a number of occasions.

Ideally, if you've asked all the right questions up front, you should come away with satisfying results. You won't need to put that guarantee into practice. You'll also have a better understanding of how to work with your chosen planner, and you'll feel more comfortable with the process. You will know when to ask questions. You will know to notify your planner when your family situation changes or new opportunities arise. You'll find that this is very much a team process. When everyone understands their role, it's easier to play together and much easier to win the game.

CHAPTER 7

When to Get Started

The trouble with answering a question such as "When do I start planning?" is that the answer might be too disheartening for some people. The ideal time to start, of course, is when your children are young. But most people don't start that early. Does that mean they are totally out of luck? Well, no. Really, there are two responses to this question. I'll start off with the answer for families with teenagers, and then I'll go into the process for families who can still take advantage of the fact that their children are still very young. You'll see that the sooner you start, the more opportunities you have in more areas than you may realize.

If you have an older child, you'll want to start your financial-aid planning before January of the student's junior year in high school. That year is called the "base year" because it is the last year that the schools don't look at in terms of your financial picture. It's past the one-year look-back period. Some schools have a two-year look-back period, but most schools have a one-year look-back period. It all depends on what that school's experience has been.

Starting When Your Child Is Young

If you have younger children, you need to start planning when they are in preschool—really as soon as possible. When I get the question "How soon should we get started?" I'll say, "Well, as soon as you find out you're having a baby." I should be the first person, aside from your spouse and your parents, you call. Here's why. The sooner you start planning, the better you'll be able to address and develop the three key aspects of this endeavor:

1. Your finances
2. Your child
3. Choosing the right college

You'll have a lot more flexibility and more choices if you plan up front and know your situation clearly every step of the way. I'll go through each aspect, and you'll see what I mean.

1. Your finances

Once you know you're going to have a child, you'll want to have a planner start doing financial projections along the way. You will need to start graphing and charting your position, just as if you were taking a journey, which you are—a life journey. You start your journey. You get married. You have your children. Your children tie into your journey. You may need a bigger vehicle to accommodate those children, or a bigger home. Everything is going to grow—your needs for retirement, their needs for an education. All of these things have to be charted and planned out. If we're working with you and if we have that plan in place, we can easily make adjustments as life changes the rules. Without a plan, it's going to be hard.

However, we do get people who come in when their child is in his or her senior year of high school. It's really hard once you start your plan because everything you do in the senior year is going to count against your financial aid. If you sell a stock, that's going to count against you because it's the year prior to you filling out the financial-aid forms. As of this writing in 2014, anything you sell in 2014 will show up on the tax return in 2015, and you will have to put that down on the FAFSA. It will hurt your chances. That's why if you're going to start making financial moves, the best time to do it is early, early, early.

It's kind of like taking medication. You go to the doctor, and he gives you medication. You need to figure out how that medication is going to affect you. You don't want to wait until your situation is so bad that now they have to put you on some sort of life-changing regimen. You want to get started with it early so you can give your doctor an opportunity to change your medication, to adjust the dosage, and to see how it affects you before it's too late.

The same thing is true with college planning. If we put a plan in place, when your child is in the fifth grade, you have seven years or so to see how that plan is working for you while having the ability to adjust it along the way. If you come in during your child's senior year, it's kind of like you're in the emergency room. You come in, and you're in critical condition. We're going to have to save your financial life or else your child can't go to college. At that point, you're left with few options. You have to do whatever you're told to do if you want to get your child through college in four years. To be honest, it may not be comfortable. I want families to have options, and that's why we have to start early.

2. Your child

When a family first comes to us in the child's senior year, certain paths are unavailable to us because of the age of the child. At that point, the child is what he is, and we can't change or morph him into the perfect candidate to fit a particular school. But when you start planning early, you have to opportunity to build that child up along the way. If I ask you, "What would you like your child to be when she grows up?" a lot of people look at me and say, "It's up to her. I just want her to be happy." That's ambiguous. It may be a true statement, but then you have to qualify it. What does it mean for her to be happy? Does it mean you want her to have a good job? Does it mean you want her to make good choices?

I have a friend who is extremely successful. One day we were talking about my son, who attends a university that ranks as one of the top schools in the world for getting a degree. My friend asked, "Harold, why your son over all the other students? What did you do that was different from everybody else?" I simply explained how I put my son on a path when he was five years old, and he never strayed from that path. It doesn't mean he's going to be happy initially on that path. I simply gave him a sense of direction early on regarding what he was supposed to be doing and then provided the resources necessary for him to stay on that path, which included but is not limited to physical and emotional support. It wasn't easy, but it was worth it.

When parents come into my office, I do quite a bit of work to understand who they are and who their children are. We're constantly helping put them on a path and then as the child progresses, we can see what their potential trajectory is, where they're going to land. Are they going to land in this field or in that field? We begin this process with our college readiness program. Our program is overseen by our academic coach/advisor, who has more than twenty-five years of experience working with students at both the high school and college levels. His expertise has proven to be instrumental. The level of care and thoroughness he provides is unmatched when it comes to helping students and parents. Upon completion of our college readiness program, students have a good idea of what kind of plan they will need to create and implement for their academic futures. They're also able to communicate that plan effectively to their parents.

We designed this service because over the years we've found that a majority of students won't have a meeting with their college or guidance counselor until their junior year of high school. This gives them very little time to plan for a major and then a career that they'll hopefully enjoy and be productive in for many years. Because this is such a daunting and intimidating task, many counselors and parents simply leave the decision up to the students. For most, being seventeen years old and having to figure out what major leads to which career or the type of options they have is extremely difficult to do. Many of them give up trying to figure it out and enter college undecided.

Roughly 80 percent of students enter college with no idea of what major they will ultimately choose. Upon entering college, they will receive very little advice. The bulk of the advice they do receive comes from their peers. It's no wonder that 50 percent of college students change their majors two to three times prior to graduating from college. Some of these students will transfer from one college to another, causing them to lose credits earned, thereby delaying graduation. This extends the length of their college stay and increases the family's overall cost by roughly $30,000 per year.

Another challenge these services were designed to avoid is the overinflated GPA. What we've seen with students from a variety of schools (public and private) is that extremely high GPAs are very common. However, the GPAs aren't measuring up. Each year, millions of students take the ACT, SAT, and SAT Subject Tests to get an idea of where they stand among their peers academically. These assessments were primarily designed to determine the level of mastery a student has over certain disciplines. Upon taking one of these exams, families are often shocked by the scores. After having some students evaluated privately, we find that there are major issues with how they are receiving their grades. Some students have gotten credit for being good students in class. Some have been able to receive extra points for making up missed assignments, even if the work isn't correct. This has led many students to have an overinflated opinion of themselves and their true ability. These issues can come to light only with private testing and are only rectified if parents and students get started early in the process.

If the child is younger, then we'll discuss early childhood development. Is the family spending money on tutoring? Are they spending money on a private school when they don't have to? Are they sending their children to the gifted and talented programs? We're looking at the investment in the child's overall future. College is important, but I share with parents that the money they invest prior to their children going off to college is what's going to save tens of thousands, if not hundreds of thousands, of dollars off the cost of the school. That's the conversation we have when parents come in, and we build their plans based on all resources that will be invested in their children. The plan has to accommodate that.

3. Choosing the right college

Another reason to begin planning early is that when you do, we can be a very effective part of the process of helping you see which colleges you should be considering for your child. Over time, we have developed a list of schools. We discuss the options with parents as they grow through this process. Let's say you come in and your child is in the fifth grade. We look at how he is doing on his national test, and then we began to plot his progress. Because we have put so much work into getting to know your child as a student, we're in the position of knowing which schools are best suited for the student, both in terms of academics and in terms of how much aid a school would be willing to give a student at a certain talent level. This is where the leveraging aspect of some schools comes into play.

In terms of how schools award money, there are schools we call "100 percent schools." They are the schools that are going to meet 100 percent of your need. Other schools are going to meet 30 to 50 percent of your need. The bottom line is that you have to know whether or not you're going to be left short on funds at a particular college before you even apply. After you get an award letter, it's pretty much too late. You're kind of at the mercy of a handful of schools. For example, if your daughter applied to seven schools and got accepted to three of them, at that point, you have three award offers, and that is all you have to go by. Should you take College 1, College 2, or College 3? How is this choice going to affect you and your child five, ten, or fifteen years down the road? depending on how you decide to pay for it? The bottom line here is that you must know these stats before you apply to those particular schools.

You should also know that often colleges use high sticker prices because it allows them wide latitude in how to use funds to attract the best students, entice students with special skills, or increase its overall racial or ethnic diversity. A report by the Pew Research Center found that although there is growing concern about escalating college prices, most Americans believe their personal investment in higher education is sound. But discounting adds complexity to decision making, deterring some students from applying. In some instances, their hesitation is based on a false sense of unaffordability. Colleges take advantage of this because the most sought-after students can be enticed by high discounts, while marginal students can be charged full price. Further, the high sticker price is a marketing tool to suggest the overall worth of a college education, along the lines of encouraging people to think that schools that cost more must provide a better education.

In essence, the best college will be the one that provides the following:

- The most free money in the form of merit and need-based aid
- The right types of majors that are obtainable in four years
- The best psychosocial fit for your student

Our services are designed to help you and your family achieve all three. However, as an integral part of the team, your student's input/communication will ultimately determine the success of our team. This is why it is extremely important to get the student involved in the positioning process as soon as possible.

What's Next?

Throughout this book, I've shared a ton of information with you. Some of it is downright frightening. Aside from losing income, the cost of a college degree is the biggest financial-plan game changer there is. Attempting to pay for college without a solid plan has spelled disaster for many families. And because the cost of a college degree has more than doubled in the past decade and is increasing at a rate higher than inflation, it seems that this difficult state of affairs will only continue. Sure, there is a lot of talk from our federal, state, and local governments about lowering the cost of college. Nowadays it's a popular message from politicians seeking election or reelection. If you ask me, they've been part of the problem and not much of the solution.

Today there are many demands for your dollar. As a matter of fact, there are only four places it can go:

- Taxes
- Purchases
- Savings or investments
- Charitable donations

With taxes, debt, and the cost of living at an all-time high in our country, how is a family supposed to get ahead and stay ahead of the rising cost of college? There are a number of things you can do, as I've discussed in this book. But remember, it all starts with a solid plan. If you don't have a plan, now would be a good time to converse with your family and create one with the help of a suitable financial planner who is well versed in the college aid process. Make sure you include your children in the conversation. When many parents create their financial plan, they have no idea how it's going to impact their children's plans because the two topics are rarely discussed simultaneously.

Now would be an excellent time to have a good talk with your children regarding money or wealth and what it means to be fiscally responsible. Let the conversation be genuine, not the usual tongue lashing that many of us probably received growing up. If you were born between 1950 and 1980, you may know what I mean.

Use this as an opportunity not only to discuss and create a plan to pay for college but also to reevaluate your other financial goals. You must be sure that your college plan, retirement plan, and estate plan are speaking the same language.

Another thing to consider is what life will look like once the children start and/or finish college. Here are a couple of questions you may use as a guide to get you started:

- Would you want to go back to college yourself to pursue the career you've always wanted? With careful planning, this could be quite doable based on how the financial-aid formulas work.
- Before planning for your children's cost of college, would it be a wise idea to meet with your parents to discuss their financial future? My charitable giving and retirement planning studies and experience reveal that many people are finding themselves in the un-

tenable situation of not only having to pay for college but also to offer financial or other assistance to their parents, especially if they are considerably older.

By the year 2025, the cost of a college degree from schools such as Stanford and Harvard will range from $100,000 to $125,000 per year. With all of the issues you'll face, only one question remains: Are you ready to pay for college in the twenty-first century? If not, you can get ready. Plenty of help is available.

I hope this book has empowered you to think about what you want and to seek the guidance that will help you get it. You can start today by visiting us at www.hgcapitaladvisors. com where you can schedule a consultation or register for one of our free college preparation strategy workshops.

About the Author

Harold A. Green is the owner of HG Capital Advisors. He has worked in Hawaii as a financial planner and consultant since 1996 with various companies. When he saw up close the need of many young students to fund their college dreams, he felt it was his calling to help parents figure out these critical issues. In 2004 Harold created HG Capital Advisors to provide college funding consulting and planning services to families faced with paying the high cost of college. He is committed to helping families send their children to college without jeopardizing their lifestyles or financial goals.

While in the US Navy, Harold was an FAA-certified air traffic controller. His years in that role taught him what it truly means to have people's lives in his hands and the importance of seeing the bigger picture of how things must fit together with precision to get travelers to their destinations safely. He now uses those principles to help parents get their children to and through college in a safe and worry-free manner.

He lives on the island of Oahu in Honolulu, Hawaii, with his wife and two children, one of whom is a student at MIT.